KT-195-327

Improving Adherence in Schizophrenia and Bipolar Disorders

Sponsored by an unrestricted educational grant from

Improving Adherence in Schizophrenia and Bipolar Disorders

MARY-JANE TACCHI
Crisis Assessment and Treatment Service, Newcastle upon Tyne, UK

and

JAN SCOTT
Institute of Psychiatry, King's College London, UK

John Wiley & Sons, Ltd

Telephone (+44) 1243 779777

Email (for orders and customer service enquiries): cs-books@wiley.co.uk
Visit our Home Page on www.wiley.com

Other Wiley Editorial Offices

John Wiley & Sons Inc., 111 River Street, Hoboken, NJ 07030, USA

Jossey-Bass, 989 Market Street, San Francisco, CA 94103-1741, USA

Wiley-VCH Verlag GmbH, Boschstr. 12, D-69469 Weinheim, Germany

John Wiley & Sons Australia Ltd, 33 Park Road, Milton, Queensland 4064, Australia

John Wiley & Sons (Asia) Pte Ltd, 2 Clementi Loop #02-01, Jin Xing Distripark, Singapore 129809

John Wiley & Sons Canada Ltd, 22 Worcester Road, Etobicoke, Ontario, Canada M9W 1L1

Wiley also publishes its books in a variety of electronic formats. Some content that appears in print may not be available in electronic books.

British Library Cataloguing in Publication Data

A catalogue record for this book is available from the British Library

ISBN-13 978-0-470-02658-8 (HB)
ISBN-10 0-470-02658-8 (HB)

Typeset in 10/12pt Palatino by Integra Software Services Pvt. Ltd, Pondicherry, India
Printed and bound in Great Britain by TJ International Ltd, Padstow, Cornwall
This book is printed on acid-free paper responsibly manufactured from sustainable forestry in which at least two trees are planted for each one used for paper production.

Contents

We gratefully acknowledge the support of an educational grant from Janssen-Cilag Ltd that allowed us to undertake the research necessary to write this book. We emphasize that the views expressed in this book are entirely our own.

We also wish to thank Linda Bell for her help (and patience) in collating references.

Mary-Jane Tacchi, Jan Scott

Part One

1

Introduction

This book explores the problem of medication non-adherence in individuals with schizophrenia and bipolar disorders. In Part One we give an overview of why this issue is of increasing concern, the nature and extent of the problem, and review a model for understanding why non-adherence occurs. In Part Two we highlight research studies of interventions that may increase treatment adherence and then outline how some of the techniques derived from these interventions can be applied in routine clinical practice. However, before undertaking these core tasks, it is important to acknowledge some of the difficulties in exploring the prevalence, predictors and potential management of non-adherence. First, the problem has largely been ignored, and until recently only about 5% of publications on treatments for schizophrenia and 1–2% of those on treatments for bipolar disorders were focused on medication non-adherence. Second, in trying to review the relevant literature it is clear that there are many different definitions of non-adherence, which obviously leads to considerable variation in how the problem and potential solutions are conceptualized. Third, studies of causes of non-adherence have often been one-dimensional, for example, focusing on the number of medications or type of side effects. If we are to begin to understand non-adherence, we need to explore what combination of variables or what sequence of events might explain why one person's behaviour may differ from that of other demographically and clinically similar individuals receiving the same treatment regime, and/or why the adherence behaviour of a person may change over time. Before discussing these topics in more detail, we give a brief review of the costs and consequences of inadequate treatment, of the terminology used, and an explanation of why this book will use the term 'adherence'.

Improving Adherence in Schizophrenia and Bipolar Disorders Mary-Jane Tacchi and Jan Scott

2

The Global Burden of Severe Mental Disorders

Until recently, the most common measure of health status was the rate of death per 1000 individuals in a defined population. However, it became increasingly obvious that this is not the most effective measure of disease burden in the population and so the World Health Organization (WHO 2003) and World Bank jointly commissioned 'The Global Burden of Disease Study' (Murray and Lopez 1996). The goal of this project was to give a more reliable and valid assessment of the burden on individuals and society associated with physical and mental health problems. Subsequently, a new measure of health status was created, the Disability Adjusted Life Year (DALY) that quantified disability, number of deaths, and the impact of premature death for a given disease in a given population. The study has proved to be very significant for mental health as it showed that the leading causes of disability are often substantially different from the leading causes of death (Murray and Lopez 1996). Across all regions of the world, mental health and neurological problems account for 10.6% of the total burden of disease, and for 28% of all DALYs, compared with 1.4% of deaths and 1.1% of years of life lost. As shown in Box 1, the burden due to these conditions is greatest in adults aged 19–45 years living in the developed world (which comprises 75% of the world population), but in terms of numbers of people affected the problem is international; and neurological/mental disorders were the most important contributor to DALYs in all regions except Sub-Saharan Africa. Furthermore, predictions for 2020 suggest most of these mental health problems will remain in the top-ten list, and the contribution of neuropsychiatric disorders is

Improving Adherence in Schizophrenia and Bipolar Disorders Mary-Jane Tacchi and Jan Scott

Box 1 The 10 leading causes of years lived with disability in 1990 (Murray and Lopez 1996)

	Total DALYs (millions)	% of total
All causes	472.7	
Unipolar major depression	50.8	10.7
Iron deficiency anaemia	22.0	4.7
Falls	22.0	4.6
Alcohol use	15.8	3.3
COPD	14.7	3.1
Bipolar disorder	14.1	3.0
Congenital anomalies	13.5	2.9
Osteoarthritis	13.3	2.8
Schizophrenia	12.1	2.6
Obsessive compulsive disorders	10.2	2.2

expected to increase to almost 15% of the global burden (Fleishman 2002).

Before considering the consequences of inadequate treatment and non-adherence in schizophrenia and bipolar disorders, it is helpful to briefly describe the epidemiology and cost of illness for these disorders.

SCHIZOPHRENIA

About 1 in 100 people will develop schizophrenia in their lifetime and the worldwide prevalence is about 2–4/1000. It affects men and women equally, although the onset in men is about five years earlier than in women (20–25 years vs 25–30 years). Acute episodes with florid symptoms may become chronic if untreated and only very rarely do the symptoms resolve spontaneously without intervention. Although medications reduce symptom severity in 70–85% of first episode cases, 60% will eventually require rehospitalization (Hayward *et al.* 1995). About 20% of patients have only one episode and experience a full remission with no impairment of function or personality, whilst about 35% go on to have several episodes with minimal impairment or between-episode remissions. A further 35% have multiple episodes with increasing levels of impairment and about 15–20% of all individuals with schizophrenia commit suicide (Cannon and Jones 1996).

Systematic reviews have demonstrated that antipsychotic medications can abort acute episodes of schizophrenia and that continuing antipsychotic drugs for at least six months reduces relapse rates compared with no treatment or placebo, and that some individuals exhibit long-term benefits from extended courses of antipsychotic medication (Fleischhacker *et al.* 2003). About 30% of people with schizophrenia are defined as having a treatment refractory disorder because, over the preceding five years, they have not had a significant reduction in symptoms, and/or they have had no period of good functioning after 2–3 regimens of standard antipsychotic medications, given at a recognized clinically effective dose for a minimum duration of six weeks each (Kane *et al.* 1992). Obviously, some of these individuals are probably non-adherent with, as opposed to non-responsive to, medication.

The estimated total cost (indirect and direct costs) of care and treatment for schizophrenia in England is over £2.6 billion, with indirect costs accounting for about 70% of this (£1.76 billion). In the US, data from cost-of-illness studies, using a variety of methodologies to calculate direct and indirect costs, have estimated that the total economic burden of schizophrenia is $32.5–49.1 billion per annum (using 1990–91 prices and assuming about two million individuals have the diagnosis). Of this total, at least $17.3 billion [35–55%] was attributed to direct medical costs (Rice 1999; Wyatt *et al.* 1995). The indirect costs vary considerably between studies, but the actual proportion of cost attributed to lost productivity [52%] and suicide [15%] are fairly constant and give some indication of the considerable economic burden associated with this disorder.

BIPOLAR DISORDERS

The lifetime prevalence of bipolar I disorder is about 1%, whilst the prevalence of bipolar spectrum disorders is about 1–5% depending on the criteria used to define the various syndromes included within this subgroup. The prevalence of bipolar I disorder does not differ in males and females, but spectrum disorders affect more women than men. The peak age of onset of bipolar I and II disorders is 15–19 years, closely followed by 20–24 years. In some patients, however, the disorder does not become manifest until they are older, or the definitive diagnosis may be delayed for 6–10 years after the occurrence of the first episode of major depression or the first symptoms or signs that the individual has a severe mental disorder.

The first episode of bipolar disorder may be manic, hypomanic, mixed or depressive, but in all cases there is very high rate of relapse and recurrence. Only about 10% of individuals achieve a full, sustained remission. Following an index episode, the cumulative probability of recurrence is about 50% by 12 months, about 70% by four years and nearly 90% by five years (Keller *et al.* 1992). Twenty-four percent of persons with bipolar disorder are rehospitalized within two years of their initial hospitalization (Hayward *et al.* 1995). Prospective follow-up studies of large cohorts of patients demonstrate that only 36% of individuals recover to their premorbid level of functioning by five years and in a 12-year follow-up employing regular symptom monitoring, Judd *et al.* (2003) showed that individuals have subsyndromal symptoms for over 50 weeks. Bipolar disorder is also associated with a significant mortality risk; about 25–40% of patients make at least one serious suicide attempt during their lives, and 11–18% will commit suicide.

The annual cost attributable to bipolar disorder in the UK is estimated to be two billion pounds (using 1991/2000 prices and assuming 297,000 people with bipolar disorder). Ten per cent of this cost (£199 million) was attributed to NHS resource use, of which 35% (£67 million) was the cost of admissions. Indirect costs comprised 86% (£1770 million) of the annual total (Das Gupta and Guest 2002) and some economic reviews suggest that bipolar disorder has the highest indirect costs of all the mental disorders. The economic burden of bipolar disorder in the US (using a lifetime prevalence rate of 1.0–1.5% and

Box 2 Epidemiology and cost of illness

	Schizophrenia	**Bipolar disorders**
General population rate	1%	1–3% (depending on criteria for spectrum disorders)
Peak age of onset (years)	Males: 20–25 Females: 25–30	15–19
Prognosis:		
Single episode with full remission	20%	10%
Multiple episodes and poor inter-episode functioning	35%	28%
Suicide rate	15–20%	11–18%
Cost of illness		
UK annual cost	£3 billion	£2 billion
Indirect cost	70% of total cost	85% of total cost

1990–91 prices) was estimated at about $30.5–45 billion per annum, of which $7 billion [16%] was direct treatment costs. One study showed the indirect treatment costs to be $38 billion, of which $17 billion was a consequence of diminished or lost productivity [45%] and $8 billion [18%] was related to lost human capital associated with suicide (Kleinman *et al*. 2003; Wyatt and Henter 1995) (Box 2).

3

The Cost and Consequences of Inadequate Treatment

This section explores the detrimental effects of non-adherence on quality of life as well as the impact on cost of services. However, the literature comprises publications on inadequate treatment, under-treatment and non-adherence with medication, and in some instances all these subgroups are combined in unknown proportions in the sample investigated. Therefore, the data must be seen as an indication of the potential adverse impact of non-adherence (Box 3). Again, we will start with an overview of the global issue, namely the 'treatment gap' in severe mental disorders, and then discuss in more detail the 'efficacy–effectiveness gap' for schizophrenia and bipolar disorders. The latter highlights specific research on non-adherence, research where it can be assumed that a significant proportion of the study sample is likely to be non-adherent, or research where the study paradigm mimics what happens when a patient becomes non-adherent (e.g. treatment trials where medication is changed from an active treatment to placebo).

THE TREATMENT GAP

A recent publication in the *Bulletin of the WHO* (Kohn 2004) explored how many individuals with mental disorders remain untreated even though effective treatments exist. The authors specifically identified community-based epidemiology studies that reported both the lifetime

Improving Adherence in Schizophrenia and Bipolar Disorders Mary-Jane Tacchi and Jan Scott

Box 3 Reported consequences of non-adherence

Schizophrenia	Bipolar disorders
Involuntary admission rates:	Relapse rates at three months:
Non-adherent = 52%	Stopped lithium = 52%
Adherent = 20%	Continued lithium = <10%
Time to admission:	Time to relapse:
Non-adherent = 10 months	Stopped antipsychotic* = 22 days
Adherent = 37 months	Continued antipsychotic* = 174 days
Relapse rates and associated annual hospital costs:	Relapse rates and associated annual hospital costs:
Non-adherent = 42%	Non-adherent = 73%
Adherent = 20%	Adherent = 31%
Non-adherent = $3500	Non-adherent = $9700
Adherent = $1800	Adherent = $3500

*Antipsychotic medication being used as a mood stabilizer.

prevalence rates for mental disorders and the data on the number of individuals currently in contact with services or receiving treatment for that specific disorder. The median treatment gap worldwide for schizophrenia and non-affective psychoses was estimated at 32%, and for bipolar disorders was 50%. Whilst the rates in Europe were lower, they were estimated at 18% and 40% respectively for schizophrenia and bipolar disorders. Although some of the untreated individuals have never attended health services or have never been offered treatment, a significant proportion of the untreated cases identified in this study are individuals who were offered treatment but then rejected the services, those who dropped out of treatment, and/or those who became non-adherent with medication. Clearly, reducing the global burden of severe mental disorders and their associated disability requires interventions that reduce this treatment gap. At a societal level there is a need to reduce barriers to seeking care by improving knowledge about mental disorders and reducing stigma. However, interventions must also be targeted at the level of the clinician–patient interaction. Many clinicians practising psychiatry in the UK will assume that the 'treatment gap' is much less in their locality, but assuming rates in line with the rest of Europe, it is possible that one to two out of every five individuals with psychosis or bipolar disorder is not being treated effectively. This increases their risk of significant morbidity and/or of mortality, increases the stress and reduces the quality of life of their significant others, and increases the global burden associated with these disorders. As undertreatment and inadequate treatment are universal, there is an urgent need to increase the involvement of clinicians in identifying individual patients with severe mental disorders who are at risk of non-adherence, as this is a treatable cause of the treatment gap. To further encourage clinicians to give more attention to the issue, we outline some of the costs and consequences of not intervening and the status quo.

THE EFFICACY–EFFECTIVENESS GAP

The efficacy of the commonly prescribed medications for schizophrenia and bipolar disorders is well established. In most randomized controlled treatment trials, antipsychotics and mood stabilizers frequently achieve remission rates of about 20–25%, response rates of 60–70% and relapse rates are reduced by 50% over 12–24 months, compared with placebo or control treatments. However, it is clear that results achieved in day-to-day clinical practice differ significantly from those reported in efficacy studies that recruit homogeneous patient populations whose interactions with clinicians are more controlled and predictable. For example, Thieda *et al.* (2003) showed that in studies of schizophrenia, non-adherence rates were about 11–33% in controlled settings, but increased to 37–57% in uncontrolled settings. Likewise, in research settings, prophylaxis with mood stabilizers reduces the risk of relapse by about 50% (from 60% to 30% on average). However, results in clinical practice are less impressive, and prophylaxis may only be fully effective in about 30% of patients with hardly any effect in about 30% of individuals (Dickson and Kendell 1986; Schou 1997). This efficacy–effectiveness gap is frequently attributed to drug pharmacokinetics and pharmacodynamics, with little attention to the influence of individual patient factors (Guscott and Taylor 1994). The latter may be overt behaviours such as comorbid substance misuse, or may be patient beliefs and attitudes that reduce the likelihood that they will adhere with medication. It is important to identify individual risk factors for non-adherence for the patients' benefit and also because of the clinical and economic consequences of the efficacy–effectiveness gap. These are now discussed separately for schizophrenia and bipolar disorders.

Schizophrenia

There are a number of studies (e.g. Rittsmannberger *et al.* 2004; Thieda *et al.* 2003) that demonstrate that non-adherence with medication in schizophrenia is associated with poor symptomatic outcome, increased risk of relapse, more frequent use of compulsory treatment (52% vs 20%) and increased risk of suicide and severe self-harm. Given the increased morbidity and mortality, it is inevitable that the cost of illness estimates are higher for individuals who are non-adherent compared to those who are adherent.

Dixon *et al.* (1997) demonstrated that, although definitions of adherence differed significantly, the general pattern of annual relapse rates showed a gradual increase, being about 23% in adherent patients in research trials compared to 50% for adherent patients in clinical practice and 70% for non-adherent patients in that setting. A meta-analysis by Weiden and Olfson (1995) demonstrated that relapse rates in individuals receiving depot medication (a proxy for full adherence) were 3.5% per month compared with 11% per month for those who were partially adherent with oral medications. Hunt *et al.* (2002) explored the relationship between clinical characteristics, adherence, and hospitalization and established a useful and clinically intuitive link. They reported that those individuals described at hospital discharge as having a 'dual diagnosis' who were non-adherent with antipsychotic medication, were readmitted to hospital within 5–6 months, as compared to about 10 months for non-adherent patients with schizophrenia alone, or adherent patients with dual diagnosis. Whereas, those patients with schizophrenia alone who adhered to medication had a median survival time of about 37 months. As Thieda *et al.* (2003) highlight in their comprehensive review of the subject, given that the hospitalization accounts for about 60–80% of the direct treatment cost (and the average cost per relapse was $9200 for a 22-day stay), these relapse rates will dramatically affect the cost of treatment for each individual. Svarstad *et al.* (2001) calculated that about 20% of regular consumers of medication were readmitted to hospital over 12 months, compared to about a 42% readmission rate in irregular consumers, and length of hospitalization (16 days vs 4 days) was also higher in irregular users compared to the regular users of medication. This translated into a mean annual cost of hospital expenditure per patient of about $1800 for regular medication users compared to $3500 for irregular users. Knapp *et al.* (2004) undertook a study of 658 patients receiving antipsychotic medication of whom about 60% [443] were diagnosed as having schizophrenia; the reported non-adherence rate was about 20%. Non-adherence was one of the most significant factors in increasing service costs, predicting an excess annual cost per patient of £2500 for inpatient services (£6714 vs £4233) and an overall additional cost of £5000 for total service use.

A recent study by Gilmer *et al.* (2004) demonstrated that both psychiatric and medical admission rates increased gradually in individuals classified as adherent, partially adherent, or non-adherent patients. Non-adherent patients also had more emergency room and clinic visits. Weiden *et al.* (2004) followed up individuals with schizophrenia for one year and demonstrated that *non-adherence conferred a greater risk of hospitalization over and above any other recognized risk factor* for readmission. There have been few studies of the impact on families of treatment non-adherence by an adult with schizophrenia. However, Clark (1994) reported that the family cost associated with dual diagnosis cases, where the individual had a severe mental illness and comorbid substance misuse (of which a significant proportion were non-adherent), was $9700–13900 compared to $2400–3500 for families whose adult children had no such chronic disorders.

Bipolar Disorders

There are a number of studies demonstrating the adverse effect of non-adherence with mood stabilizers, particularly lithium, on clinical outcomes and attempted or completed suicide. There are fewer published studies of the cost of illness for individuals with bipolar disorders who are adherent or non-adherent with medications, but the findings are similar to those reported for schizophrenia. Examples of these studies are reviewed as follows.

Retrospective studies (e.g. Mander 1986) have repeatedly highlighted that rapid discontinuation of lithium is associated with a high risk of manic relapse in the first three months after stopping the medication [50%], compared with relapses in individuals receiving ongoing prophylaxis [<10%]. These findings parallel clinical studies such as those by Keck *et al.* (1997; 1998) that demonstrated that 60–80% of individuals hospitalized with a manic episode were non-adherent with prescribed mood stabilizers in the month immediately prior to admission. There are no similar studies of the impact of stopping anticonvulsants when used as mood stabilizers, but there is a recent study that gives some indication of the likely effect of stopping antipsychotic prophylaxis in bipolar disorders. A randomized controlled trial allocated patients to continued treatment with atypical antipsychotics or a switch from active treatment to placebo. Forty percent of individuals receiving ongoing antipsychotic treatment experienced a relapse, compared with 80% of those who swapped from antipsychotic medication (given during the acute episode) to placebo treatment during the prophylaxis phase of the study (Tohen *et al.* 2005). The time to any type of mood episode was only 22 days in the placebo group compared to 174 days in those receiving the active medication. However, the significant differences in relapses were almost entirely accounted for by the increased rate of manic relapses, and the effect of stopping prophylaxis on risk of depressive relapse remains uncertain (Franks *et al.* 2005). Whilst these studies do not directly assess the effect of adherence or non-adherence, they offer an indication of the potential impact of irregular use or non-adherence with medication.

There are relatively few prospective studies in this field, but Scott and Pope (2002a) explored the relationship between medication adherence, plasma levels of mood stabilizers and psychiatric hospitalizations in 98 individuals with mood disorders. Thirty-two percent of subjects reported partial adherence with prophylaxis whilst about 50% of subjects were regarded as adherent. At 18 months, 27 out of 92 individuals experienced one or more admissions. Whilst the cumulative probability of admission was 29%, admission rates were significantly higher in partially adherent subjects with sub-therapeutic plasma levels (about 80%) than adherent subjects with therapeutic plasma levels (about 10%).

There is no definitive data of any association between adherence rates and mortality. However, Muller-Oerlinghausen and colleagues (1996; 2001) have published a series of papers that demonstrate that continuous use of lithium may reduce the risk of attempted or actual suicide, and that stopping lithium increases the risk of death from suicide or other physical disorders, particularly cardiovascular disorders. Their largest collaborative study of over 5500 patient years showed that adequate long-term lithium treatment significantly reduced and even normalized the excess mortality rates found in patients with mood disorders. They also demonstrated a significant reduction of suicide attempts per year as compared to a corresponding pre-lithium period (0.10 vs 0.33 attempts p.a.). Furthermore, a meta-analysis on 17,000 patients pooled from 28 studies demonstrated that the rate of suicidal acts is 8.6-fold higher in patients not receiving long-term lithium, as compared to those with regular lithium treatment. Whilst this data is widely seen as showing the benefits of long-term lithium use, it only offers indirect evidence of the potential benefits of adherence with mood stabilizers as: (i) not all the subjects incorporated into the 'discontinued' from lithium or 'not receiving' long-term treatment groups will have been non-adherent; and (ii) there is no data on the effects of partial adherence with lithium or evaluating the effect of combined therapies versus lithium monotherapy. Nevertheless, these publications have been widely seen as advocating the importance of sustained prophylaxis. It remains to be seen whether any of the newer mood stabilizers have an equivalent protective effect, as no similar studies are available as yet.

There are no UK publications on mood stabilizers comparable with the Knapp *et al.* (2004) study on antipsychotics, but a number of researchers in the US have estimated the costs of illness in adherent and non-adherent patients or in those with complex bipolar disorders. Svarstad *et al.* (2001) reported 33% of individuals with bipolar disorders were irregular users of medication. Hospitalization rates were 73% for those classified as irregular users compared with 31% for regular users. The average length of hospitalization was considerably longer, being 37 days for irregular users and 4 days for regular users of medication, leading to highly significant differences in hospital costs of $9701 in irregular users compared with $1657 in regular medication users. Interestingly, a case series reported by Durrenberger *et al.* (1999) demonstrated that over six years the cost of care for a non-adherent patient with frequent manic relapses (about $4000 per month) was equal to that for *13* individuals who were adherent with their mood stabilizers ($320 per month). Begley *et al.* (2001) suggest the cost of care for chronic unresponsive bipolar disorders (often characterized by comorbid substance misuse and non-adherence) was about $264,785 per person compared to $11720 for an individual who experiences only a single manic episode. Lastly, Wyatt *et al.* (2001) estimated that the regular use of lithium saves about eight billion dollars per year of which about one billion dollars is direct treatment cost.

4

A Note on Terminology: Compliance, Adherence and Concordance

A major stumbling block for coordinated research in this field is the unresolved debate about how best to define patient engagement with or acceptance of a treatment regime (Myers and Midence 1998). Until the 1980s most work on patient engagement with medication regimes was described as compliance. This expression is still widely employed in the research literature, but it has fallen out of favour in clinical practice in the UK because of the increasing concern that the term 'compliance' carries an assumption that patients are passive recipients of the doctors' 'words of wisdom' (no matter how well intentioned) and that the clinician is always in a position of authority. As such, compliance implies that the patient should follow their doctors' advice without question, focuses primarily on only one aspect of treatment (namely medication) and equates non-compliance with 'behaving badly' (Hamann *et al.* 2003). In recent years there has been a shift away from this paternalistic model of doctor–patient interactions with the consequent preference for the use of the term 'adherence', with others going further still and advocating that the focus should be on 'concordance' (McGavock 1996).

Noble (1998) explored the concept of adherence in detail and highlighted why this began to gain favour. She noted that patients using modern health systems are more active in their own health care, bringing a complex agenda to the doctor rather than a simple 'medico-centric' view of their illness. Noble suggests that treatment regimes are modified

Improving Adherence in Schizophrenia and Bipolar Disorders Mary-Jane Tacchi and Jan Scott

or distorted by the consumer (leading to partial adherence) rather than being completely accepted or totally abandoned. Thus, the notion of adherence incorporates the idea that this behaviour is in a dynamic state and may change over time. Full adherence as a 'default setting' with non-adherence as the only alternative behaviour is too simplistic as it fails to reflect the clinical reality or take into account the patient's changing perceptions of their problem. An individual's pattern of adherence is best viewed as a 'spectrum behaviour' and is likely to vary on a continuum between individuals and also change in any given individual over time. As such, it is clear that both patients and professionals will be responsible for regularly reviewing adherence status and revising their 'contract' in order to maintain the patients' engagement with and acceptance of treatment.

The turn of the century has seen a number of changes in perceptions of mental disorder, treatment approaches and goals, and mental health care systems (Fenton 2003). For example, the wide availability of information on the internet and through other sources means that individuals frequently develop quite sophisticated ideas on the nature of their problems and the most appropriate solution from their perspective prior to consultation with a health professional. Indeed this information gathering, analysis, and the personal values of that individual may dictate whether they chose to consult a clinician at all. Furthermore, the philosophy of expert patients and patient–professional partnerships has been increasingly promoted by advocacy groups and is now incorporated into government policy in the UK (Palmer and Scott 2004). These developments, plus the shift to a view that many mental and physical disorders are 'life course illnesses' with recurrences and remissions rather than isolated acute episodes, have led to a change in the goals of treatment from the notion of 'cure' to that of disease management (WHO 2003). These and other issues have led to an increased emphasis on active participation by and equal responsibility allotted to the individuals involved in the therapeutic relationship. These are not only key components of concordance, but also promote the idea that the patient and professional may legitimately hold differing ideas about what would be the appropriate treatment intervention and that the management of any symptoms or disorder will require negotiation (Hamann *et al.* 2003). So, concordance carries with it the expectation that clinicians will offer respect, information, and choice to the individual and that the doctor should ensure they understand and acknowledge the patient's unique personal priorities or concerns. This aspect is relatively incontentious, as it describes many of the ideal components of a good doctor–patient interaction. However, there is some confusion in the literature about whether concordance represents a step beyond adherence. It has been highlighted that the concept (theoretically) implies that the clinician could be expected to prescribe a treatment purely on the basis of patient preference, rather than offering the individual the option of selecting their preferred treatment from a more restricted, but evidence-based range of interventions. It can be argued that providing a prescription purely on the basis of patient preference would achieve a high level of adherence, but if that treatment has limited benefits it would be hard for most clinicians to concur with this approach. As such, whilst clinicians accept the principles of concordance, there are still aspects of this approach to consultations that are not currently incorporated into routine practice.

To avoid further confusion about terminology, for the purposes of this text we will adopt the position that concordance describes the *process* of the consultation, whilst *adherence* describes a possible (successful) outcome of that process. In the second part of this book we explore how to promote a balanced therapeutic alliance and how clinicians can incorporate the key elements of concordance into their clinical work.

The literature review in Part One of this book we will use the term 'adherence', as it appears to most accurately reflect the target behaviour. Whilst this concept is not as focused on the patient–professional relationship as concordance, it emphasizes that, unlike compliance, clinicians play an important role in promoting a therapeutic alliance and providing relevant information, and recognizes the active rather than passive participation of the patient in this process (Frank *et al.* 1992). A succinct and acceptable definition of adherence is 'patient acceptance of and engagement in healthy behaviours' (Wright 1993). As shown in Box 4, this definition may include attendance at consultations and engagement in a healthy lifestyle, as well as taking any prescribed medications in the appropriate doses at the appropriate time of day for the recommended duration (WHO 2003). The definition also implies that other potentially harmful behaviours, such as abuse or excessive use of prescribed medication without lethal

Box 4 Defining adherence

Adherence
The extent to which a person's behaviour—taking medication, following a diet, and/or executing lifestyle changes—corresponds with agreed recommendations from a healthcare provider.

intention (Buckley *et al.* 1991), would also constitute non-adherence. The flaw in this brief definition of adherence is that it fails to acknowledge that 'non-adherence' is rarely an all or nothing phenomenon (Goodwin and Jamison 1990), but this issue will be emphasized at different points in the book.

5

Measuring Adherence

The problem of terminology in adherence research is compounded by the difficulty of making a reliable and valid estimate of adherence status. The methods used to measure non-adherence have been wide-ranging and the actual approach employed is partly dictated by the setting in which measurement takes place, the financial and personal resources available to undertake the assessment, and the acceptable response burden placed on the patient (WHO 2003).

As shown in Box 5, subjective methods include examining case-note recordings, direct patient interviews, obtaining collateral reports from clinicians or significant others, and noting the attending physicians' clinical judgement about adherence. Interestingly, the latter is only 50% reliable (Gilbert *et al.* 1980). Both patients and clinicians tend to over-estimate adherence, but patient self-report may actually be the most accurate subjective method (Stephenson *et al.* 1993). Although it suffers from low sensitivity (about 50%), it generally has high specificity [90%]. For example, in a recent study of non-adherence with mood stabilizers, self-reports of missing more than 30% of prescribed medication over a month were highly correlated with independently assessed serum lithium levels (Scott and Pope 2002). Stephenson *et al.* (1993) calculated that patients tend to overestimate adherence by about 17%, whereas the variability between clinicians assessing the same patient is considerably greater. The accuracy of subjective methods may be improved by using a combination of patient, significant other, and clinician judgement to detect non-adherence (e.g. Adams and Scott 2000; Colom *et al.* 2000).

Objective methods of assessing adherence include: monitoring rates of dispensing of repeat prescriptions; counting the number of tablets

Improving Adherence in Schizophrenia and Bipolar Disorders Mary-Jane Tacchi and Jan Scott

Box 5 Measuring medication adherence

Subjective Measurements	Objective Measurements
Case-note recordings	Pill count
Collateral reports from clinicians or significant others	Monitoring dispensing of repeat prescriptions
Clinical judgment	Cumulative possession ratio
Direct patient interviews	Serum drug or metabolite levels
Questionnaire ratings	Estimating the L/D ratio
	Analysis of urine for drugs or their metabolites
	Electronic event monitoring

left in pill bottles (to give a proportion of medication doses missed either as a percentage or as a number of days or weeks); cumulative possession ratios (the number of days medication is available for consumption divided by the number of days subjects were eligible to receive medication from an insurer or pharmacy; for example, a person collecting 240 days supply who is eligible for the entire year of treatment has a cumulative possession ratio of 0.66); monitoring of serum drug levels; estimating the ratio of the plasma drug level and the administered dose (L/D ratio); analysis of urine for drugs or their metabolites; and electronic event monitoring systems which record every occasion that a pill bottle is opened.

Although preferable to subjective methods in many respects, objective methods do pose problems concerning the time of ingestion of medication and measurement of drug levels, and of pharmacokinetic variability. These methods are usually more expensive than interview-based approaches and there can be issues in obtaining and matching individual data from more than one computer or source (e.g. as required to calculate cumulative possession ratios), and about obtaining informed consent from a patient who may already be non-adherent. Methods based around records of collection or filling of scripts are probably the least expensive objective methods. However, about 5% of patients never take a prescription to be dispensed at all (Scott 1999), and rates of failure to refill a script tend to increase over time. These approaches would give an indication of those individuals who are totally non-adherent (i.e. rare cases from one end of the spectrum). Other objective techniques have different weaknesses: for example, the difficulty with monitoring of antidepressant and antipsychotic medication levels in plasma and urine are that they show considerable inter-individual variation (Altamura and Mauri 1985; Velligan *et al.* 2003). Specific to lithium monitoring, opinions differ as to the value of measuring plasma levels alone or the ratio of lithium concentration in red blood cells (RBC) to serum levels (Gengo *et al.* 1980). Alternatively, Harvey and Peet (1991) recommend using serial measures of RBC lithium levels during a fixed dosage regime to measure changes in adherence (using the L/D ratio). A recent study suggests simply calculating the mean variation in lithium level over time, as stability of the plasma level may be a better indicator of adherence rather than fluctuating levels (Scott 2000). These methods are still fallible, as patients can take 'loading doses' of medication prior to blood tests. Even expensive methods such as the electronic monitoring of how many occasions and at what time of day a pill bottle is opened can be unreliable if the patient chooses not to swallow the medication that was removed.

As all these assessments give an estimate of the patient's behaviour rather than a definitive measurement of adherence, the current state of the art usually involves a combination of approaches: for example patient self-report and plasma levels or self-report and event monitoring.

6

A Few Myths about Non-Adherence

There are a number of myths that need to be dispelled about non-adherence with treatment in individuals with mental disorders. These misunderstandings can be summarized as follows: non-adherence is more common in mental disorders as compared with physical disorders; demographic factors (e.g. being young, single and male) identify individuals who are non-adherent with prescribed medication; and side effects are the major cause of non-adherence.

In reviews that specifically explore non-adherence across a number of persistent health problems (Haynes *et al.* 1979; WHO 2003), it has been consistently demonstrated that the average rate of non-adherence in individuals prescribed long-term treatments was about 30–40% (Box 6). Physical health problems such as diabetes, hypertension, and renal disorders have similar non-adherence rates and these are about the same as those reported for mental disorders. A meta-analysis by Cramer and Rosenheck (1999) reported that rates of adherence with antipsychotics [60%] and antidepressants [68%] were not significantly different than those of a variety of non-psychiatric medications [58%–78%].

The early literature on adherence was restricted to the study of demographic and basic clinical factors that might be associated with poor adherence. Although some associations were found, the limited number of potential predictors that were included in the analyses undermined the reliability of these isolated findings. When Haynes *et al.* (2002) undertook a comprehensive review of 185 studies, they failed to establish any robust relationship between adherence and any of the following: gender, social class or occupation, marital status, educational

Improving Adherence in Schizophrenia and Bipolar Disorders Mary-Jane Tacchi and Jan Scott

Box 6 Important facts about adherence in all disorders

1. Rates of non-adherence with medication in persistent mental disorders average about 30%, the same rate as reported for chronic physical disorders.
2. An individual's adherence status usually changes over time, but total adherence or total non-adherence are rare patterns of behaviour.
3. Non-adherence rates have remained static for about 40 years despite the introduction of new medications with more benign side-effect profiles. Side effects are unlikely to be the key factor in explaining why an individual is non-adherent.

attainment, intelligence level or ethnicity. Although some of the studies have found an association between adherence and gender, the amount of variance explained is very small. Also, as it has become clearer that an individual's adherence status may vary over time, it makes sense that changes in the patients' beliefs or experiences of treatment are more likely to explain their behaviour rather than categorical, static factors such as membership of a demographically defined subpopulation.

The final misunderstanding is that there is a direct and all-encompassing correlation between adherence status and concrete measures of number or severity of side effects. These are important, but only rarely do they offer a full explanation for non-adherence. For example, most clinicians can quickly identify individuals from their caseload who experience distressing side effects that may cause that person to reject a prescribed treatment. However, they will also know individuals who adhere to medication and tolerate quite marked objective side effects and other patients who fail to adhere despite a lack of subjective reports or objective evidence of side effects. The marketing literature distributed by pharmaceutical companies often suggests differential rates of non-adherence between medications X and Y that are then linked directly to their different side-effect profiles. However, the available research suggests any association is complex; a review of data published over the last few decades that explore a range of influences on adherence indicate that non-adherence rates have remained static despite the introduction of a number of new medications with apparently more benign side-effect profiles. Objective examinations of the prevalence of side effects demonstrate only a weak association between current side effects and adherence (Gray *et al.* 2002;

Scott and Pope 2002). Furthermore, in individuals with schizophrenia and physical health problems, rates of treatment non-adherence with medication for physical disorders parallel the rates of non-adherence with anti-psychotics (Dolder *et al.* 2003). Given significant differences in the pharmacological profile of these medications, their benefits and sites of action, it is difficult to provide a rationale for this pattern of behaviour simply on the basis of side effects. As will be discussed in the coming sections, this suggests that a straightforward cause-and-effect model cannot be advocated when explaining the relationship between psychotropic medication side effects and adherence status.

7

Overview of Prevalence and Predictors of Adherence

SCHIZOPHRENIA

Prevalence

Antipsychotic medications are the most widely used treatment for schizophrenia. Rates of non-adherence with all types of antipsychotics reported over the past four decades range from 20% to 89% with a median of about 50% (Fenton *et al.* 1997) depending on the criteria used for assessing adherence and whether the samples comprised only of patients with schizophrenia or included all forms of psychosis. The prescribing of atypicals now exceeds that of typical antipsychotics in the UK, but the latter are still used frequently. Oral medications make up 80% of prescriptions (Valenstein *et al.* 2001). There has been a reduction in the use of depot medications over the last 15 years, possibly because, until recently, most of the atypicals were only available in oral forms.

In 39 studies included in a systematic review of psychosis, the overall weighted mean rate of medication non-adherence in over 6000 subjects was 30% (Barbui and Tansella 2003); slightly higher than the rate of non-adherence defined as dropouts from treatment follow-up (total number of subjects = 20,000; dropout rate = 26%). More recent studies have used different approaches to defining non-adherence in schizophrenia such as the number of days of medication missed by individuals receiving repeated prescriptions. Olfson *et al.* (2000) reported that 20% of patients miss one or more consecutive weeks of treatment over three months. Kane (2003) defined the level of adherence according to

Improving Adherence in Schizophrenia and Bipolar Disorders Mary-Jane Tacchi and Jan Scott

whether an individual took less than 25% prescribed medication (complete non-adherence), 25–65% (partial adherence), or more than 65% (adherent). Using these criteria, Rettenbacher *et al.* (2004) reported rates of complete and partial non-adherence of 8% and 39% respectively, whilst 53% of patients took over 65% of their prescribed antipsychotic medications. However, as Mahmoud *et al.* (2004) showed, this might change over time and non-adherence affects almost all patients to some extent at some point during treatment. Gilmer *et al.* (2004) reported that 19% of individuals with schizophrenia were non-adherent because they were 'excess fillers', a term describing individuals who request additional prescriptions for their recommended medications (i.e. they have a cumulative possession ratio >1.1).

For those recently commenced on medication, early discontinuation (7–10 days) may occur in as many as 25% of patients, reaching about 50% by the end of 12 months (Velligan *et al.* 2003). Similar rates (40% at one year) are reported for non-adherence or dropout from treatment in subjects with first episode psychosis attending a specialist early psychosis service in Canada (Coldham *et al.* 2002). Interestingly, although adherence to atypical antipsychotics may be marginally better than typicals in the short term, there is no evidence that these differences persist: earlier research suggesting greater adherence with the atypicals than the typicals has not been replicated in recent more systematic studies undertaken by independent investigators in naturalistic settings (Valenstein *et al.* 2001; Velligan *et al.* 2003). There is a possibility that individuals on atypicals may switch to other medications less frequently than those prescribed typical antipsychotics (Menzin *et al.* 2003).

About 50% of individuals are reported to be non-adherent with depot antipsychotics (Curson *et al.* 1985), although this treatment is often offered to those who struggle to adhere with prescribed medications, and in one study 49% of those offered depot medication had been non-adherent with oral medications in the previous year (Valenstein *et al.* 2001). Interestingly, Weiden *et al.* (1996) found no difference over 12 months in adherence rates with oral or depot medication.

Predictors

Barbui and Tansella (2003) undertook a systematic review of earlier publications on putative predictors of medication adherence or regular outpatient attendance. Few of the studies included in the review explored more subtle personal attitudes or contextual factors such as family environment, or looked at which combination of factors accounted significantly for the variance in adherence level. As such, it is not surprising that, like previous publications (e.g. Buchanan 1992), the review largely endorsed a predictable checklist of features associated with non-adherence, i.e. being young, male, and unemployed or socially isolated, with a past history of non-adherence and possibly currently using illicit substances. However, it is noteworthy that another large-scale review by Lacro *et al.* (2002) found no association between age, gender, and adherence.

As might be expected, adherence was shown to be greater in those in regular contact with services (Rittmannsberger *et al.* 2004), and in those whose medication is being monitored closely, for example because they are taking clozapine (Gilmer *et al.* 2004), whilst non-adherence may be more frequent in those receiving a higher number of doses of medication per day (Diaz *et al.* 2001). Non-adherence may reduce somewhat with age (Gilmer *et al.* 2004) but this may be balanced by the higher rates of non-adherence in those with cognitive deficits (Robinson *et al.* 2002; Diaz *et al.* 2001). Interestingly, Jeste *et al.* (2003) showed that impairments in conceptualization skills and memory were particularly significant predictors of poorer medication management ability.

The above review highlights the problems of contradictory findings, for example about age and adherence, that may be reported when potential predictors of adherence are researched, or the relationship of each variable to adherence level is analysed separately, rather than in combination with other factors that may provide a more in-depth analysis of the underlying causes of or reasons for non-adherence. The studies quoted below exemplify research exploring individual or family beliefs or attitudes, treatment setting or doctor–patient interactions as well as core clinical or demographic factors. Studies that model statistically how combinations of variables may predict adherence are also noted.

When attitudinal and clinical factors are explored together, negative attitudes to medication and relative lack of insight or illness awareness were the variables that contributed significantly to the variance in adherence levels, particularly in the early stages of treatment (Mutsatsa *et al.* 2003). It is important to note that although poorly adherent patients also had higher levels of psychopathology, more frequent medication side effects, a greater prevalence of substance misuse and a lower subjective sense of well-being, these factors did not significantly predict adherence when they were included in a regression analysis with the other putative predictors. Loffler and colleagues (2003) also explored subjective reasons for adherence or non-adherence and the stability of these views over time. They found that persistent ideas that predicted non-adherence were lack of acceptance of the necessity for medication, subjectively distressing side effects, and impaired insight. In contrast, adherent subjects reported greater perceived daily benefits of treatment, a positive therapeutic relationship, and were more likely to have a significant other who expressed a positive attitude towards the use of medication. Interestingly, Sajatovic *et al.* (2002) found that the attitudes of individuals towards medication, whether predominantly positive or negative, remained relatively stable during the course of inpatient treatment despite improvements in insight and reductions in symptoms. Like a number of other studies (Dolder *et al.* 2002; Donohue *et al.* 2001; Freudenreich *et al.* 2004; Hofer *et al.* 2002; Kemp and David 1996), Sajatovic and colleagues (2002) also noted that negative attitudes to medication significantly predicted non-adherence. Hattenschwiler *et al.* (2003) found that trust in medication and having a healthy locus of control that endorsed 'powerful others' (beliefs such as 'I can rely on a good clinician') were significant predictors of medication adherence six weeks after discharge from an acute admission unit, whilst poor adherence was predicted by guilt, idiosyncratic beliefs (including aversion to medication) and an internal locus of control (beliefs such as 'I know I can help myself'). Vauth *et al.* (2004) used confirmatory factor analysis to identify three dimensions (from a model proposed by Weiden *et al.* 1994) that together predicted adherence behaviour namely the influence of others, medication affinity, and belief in the importance of relapse prevention.

Linden *et al.* (2001) found that adherent patients rated themselves as having higher positive treatment expectations and were identified by their clinicians at the outset of treatment as being more cooperative. Lambert *et al.* (2004) noted that whilst side effects, even those regarded as distressing because of the physical (e.g. akathisia) or psychological consequences (e.g. sexual dysfunction), did not directly predict adherence, they were associated with an increased likelihood of negative attitudes towards medication. This suggests that side effects may contribute indirectly to the variance in non-adherence in certain circumstances; an idea that receives some support from other publications. For example, subjective reports of concerns about side effects may predict adherence in some individuals even when their objective level of side effects does not predict this behaviour (Gray *et al.* 2002). Furthermore, a qualitative analysis suggested that patients do not necessarily differentiate symptoms and side effects per se, but when asked about their views they tend to describe medications in global terms such as 'good or terrible', i.e. the individual's chosen descriptor gives an indication of the total impact (benefits outweigh negative consequences, or vice versa) of the treatment (Carrick *et al.* 2004). Likewise, in a study of just under 1000 patients, a global measure of satisfaction with treatment was found to significantly predict adherence (Gasquet *et al.* 2003).

There is virtually no data regarding personality traits that may be associated with increased risk of non-adherence in individuals with schizophrenia; one of the few papers on the topic (Liraud and Verdoux 2001) found a link between non-adherence and sensation seeking, disinhibition, and boredom susceptibility. Perceived threat to freedom of choice (Moore *et al.* 2000), viewing schizophrenia as less severe than physical disorders such as diabetes or epilepsy (Rettenbacher *et al.* 2004a), lack of family support (Coldham *et al.* 2002) or high levels of expressed emotion (EE) in family members (Sellwood *et al.* 2003) have all been found to predict non-adherence in independent studies. McCabe and Priebe (2004) showed that ethnic groups who supported biological rather than social or spiritual explanations of causation reported greater treatment satisfaction and better therapeutic relationships, but only non-significantly different medication adherence rates. Holzinger *et al.* (2002) reported that, although subjective illness theory (patients' views on diagnosis, aetiology and prognosis) did not directly predict adherence, the patients' views of the helping alliance with the clinicians and their attitudes towards drugs did predict likelihood of medication adherence. Nelson *et al.* (1983) noted that the patient's perception of the clinician's interest in them as a person also predicted adherence. Indeed, it seems that therapeutic alliance is one of the most robust predictors of adherence. For example, non-adherence in individuals after a recent acute hospitalization was predicted by poor therapeutic alliances with staff and a greater likelihood that their family had refused to be involved in their treatment (Olfson *et al.* 2000). Interestingly, Weiss *et al.* (2002) found that positive therapeutic alliance actually predicted the time taken to move from being non-adherent to becoming adherent (5–6 months).

There are hardly any publications of predictors of non-adherence with depot medication, but recent studies (e.g. Patel *et al.* 2004; Tattan and Creed 2001; Valenstein *et al.* 2001) indicate that individuals being prescribed depot medications tend to receive higher doses of antipsychotics than those prescribed oral medication and reported more side effects. Of these individuals, those with negative symptoms or who experienced persistent, treatment refractory symptoms were most likely to become non-adherent.

Box 7 identifies those factors for which there is consistent evidence of an association with non-adherence or where there are more positive than negative findings of an association.

Box 7 Predictors of non-adherence in schizophrenia

Basic demographic, illness or treatment factors
Living alone
Comorbid substance misuse
Short duration of disorder
Long duration of disorder or treatment
Past history of non-adherence
Cognitive impairments
Lack of insight
More frequent dosing
Subjective experience of side effects

Individual, family or patient–professional relationship factors
High EE family
Lack of illness awareness
Internal locus of control
Poor therapeutic alliance
Negative expectations of or attitudes towards treatment

BIPOLAR DISORDERS

Prevalence

Mood stabilizers such as lithium, valproate, and carbamazepine are the mainstay of treatment of severe recurrent affective disorders. Reported non-adherence rates for long-term prophylaxis range from 20% to 66% (Bech *et al.* 1976; Scott 2000), with a median prevalence of 41%. In a large-scale study of over 1500 patients, Johnson and McFarland (1998) reported that the median duration of continuous use of lithium after it was first prescribed was about two months (76 days). Schumann *et al.* (1999) reported that 43% of individuals receiving prophylactic lithium were non-adherent for six months. Jamison *et al.* (1979) also noted that over a two-year follow-up period, use of prophylactic medication was often intermittent, with 50% of patients with bipolar disorders stopping and re-starting their lithium at least once and 30% at least twice. Similar rates were reported in clinical and community surveys (Scott and Pope 2002; Morselli and Elgie 2003). The largest study of subjects prescribed carbamazepine and valproate ($n = 140$) reported non-adherence rates in the maintenance phase of treatment of over 50% (Keck *et al.* 1997).

There are no studies exploring adherence separately for those receiving treatment for unipolar as compared to bipolar depressive episodes. Research on adherence with antidepressants suggest that 40% of individuals discontinue medication within 12 weeks (Peveler *et al.* 2000) and Katon *et al.* (1992) reported that only 20–34% of individuals filled four or more prescriptions for antidepressants. The pooled data analyzed by Cramer and Rosenheck (1999) suggest that adherence rates for antidepressants rarely exceed 65%.

Predictors

There are a number of review articles (Colom and Vieta 2002; Goodwin and Jamison 1990; Lingham and Scott 2002) that identify possible sociodemographic and general clinical predictors of non-adherence in bipolar disorders. The most commonly identified factors in early reviews were: first year of lithium treatment, past history of non-adherence, younger age, male gender, fewer episodes of illness, history of grandiosity, elevated mood, and complaints of 'missing highs'.

As noted in the review of schizophrenia, the hypothesis that basic sociodemographic variables directly predict adherence is not strongly supported by recent studies or is undermined by contradictory findings. For example, five studies identified a possible association between younger age and non-adherence, one found a trend in the same direction but six studies have not found an association (Perlick *et al.* 2004). Side effects were considered to have a detrimental effect on adherence in an early study by Jamison and Akiskal (1983), but again the difference between subjective and objective measures of side effects seems to be important, as Scott and Pope (2002b) demonstrated that *fear of* rather than *actual* side effects was a significant predictor of non-adherence. A detailed review of the relationship between mania and adherence suggests that non-adherence actually becomes a significant problem during the prodromal stages of an acute episode occurring in 60–80% of subjects in the month prior to hospitalization (Keck *et al.* 1998). However, this does not prove the direction of causality, as non-adherence may lead to mania or having symptoms of mania may increase the likelihood of non-adherence. Despite this association, those who have a past history of frequent episodes of mania are not necessarily more at risk of non-adherence (e.g. Schumann *et al.* 1999) and an alternative explanation of non-adherence is that those with more episodes of mania have higher levels of cognitive impairment (Ferrier *et al.* 1999).

The most important additional risk factor to emerge in research over the last decade is the association between non-adherence and comorbid drug and/or alcohol misuse (e.g. Keck *et al.* 1997; Swartz *et al.* 1998). Other studies have highlighted the importance of lack of insight, lack of illness awareness, and cognitive deficits in increasing the risk of non-adherence in bipolar disorders (Danion 1987; Schumann *et al.* 1999; Trauer and Sacks 2000). Also, Jamison and Akiskal (1983) suggested that certain personality traits might predict non-adherence and the importance of comorbid personality dysfunction has been confirmed in recent studies (e.g. Colom *et al.* 2000). Although there is a paucity of research on predictors of adherence with antidepressants, it is noteworthy that personality traits known to be highly prevalent in individuals with bipolar disorders appear to predict lower levels of adherence with antidepressants. For example, Ekselius *et al.* (2000) reported that sensation-seeking personality traits were associated with lower serum levels of antidepressants (but not self-reported adherence levels) and Cohen *et al.* (2004) found that extraversion was a significant negative predictor of adherence. The latter study also reported that symptom severity and side effects were not predictors of adherence.

In an attempt to explore underlying beliefs and expectations, Jamison *et al.* (1979) asked 42 patients treated with lithium to identify in rank order the reasons for their non-adherence. Two of the most frequently endorsed reasons were that patients disliked the idea that their moods were controlled by medication and disliked taking medication as it reminded them that they had a chronic illness. Pope and Scott (2003) confirmed the importance of these two constructs and also found that many patients reported that when they felt well they thought there was no need to take medication. This belief may explain the association between a greater length of time on a mood stabilizer also predicted non-adherence (Scott and Pope 2002b). Cochran (1984), similarly noted that patients attending a lithium clinic expressed concerns about the course of the illness, distress about being a 'chronic mental patient', discomfort about the psychosocial changes that they attributed to lithium, and anxieties about the safety of long-term lithium treatment.

Other studies suggest that patients who express a strong belief that they should personally try harder to control their illness were less likely to adhere (Cochran 1984; Scott 1995). In contrast, those patients reporting concerns about the perceived adverse consequences and threat of the illness and those able to recognize the benefits of treatment, were more likely to adhere (Adams and Scott 2000; Swatz *et al.* 1998). Greenhouse and colleagues (2000) and Scott (2000) also discuss the role of denial of severity of disorder in increasing the risk of non-adherence.

These findings have some parallels with those reported by Connelly *et al.* (1982) who found that demographic factors and health beliefs predicted about a 20% variance in adherence to lithium, and of Keck and colleagues (1997; 1998) who found that the most common reason for non-adherence was denial of need.

Scott (2000) reported a factor analysis of the dimensions of adherence behaviour using the same measures employed in research in schizophrenia (Weiden *et al.* 1994). This confirmed that medication affinity and relapse prevention were important predictors of adherence and that negative interactions with clinicians was reported four times more frequently in non-adherent as compared with adherent subjects. Likewise, Kleindienst and Greil (2004) reported that trust in the treating clinician, trust in the medication and more positive expectations of treatment were associated with longer duration of adherence.

Cochran and Gitlin (1988) found that patients' attitudes towards taking lithium were strongly influenced by the views of significant others, and that individuals with bipolar disorders who believed their

Box 8 Predictors of non-adherence in bipolar disorders

Basic demographics, illness or treatment factors
Comorbid substance misuse
Short duration of disorder
Long duration of treatment
Past history of non-adherence
Cognitive impairments
Lack of insight
Subjective experience of side effects

Individual, family or patient–professional relationship factors
Fear of side effects
Lack of illness awareness
Internal locus of control
Poor therapeutic alliance
Negative expectations of or attitudes towards treatment
Knowledge and beliefs of significant others
High EE family
Negative ideas about taking long-term medication because, for example, it repeatedly reminded the person that the disorder is chronic; and they develop concerns about being 'controlled by drugs'

family and friends thought they should take lithium were significantly more likely to be adherent than those who did not hold this belief. Their study also highlighted the importance of the attitudes of the treating physician. In a study from India, abnormal illness concepts reported by the significant others of a patient were associated with delayed help-seeking, and more adaptive illness concepts in significant others increased the likelihood they would actively participate in treatment decisions and that the patient would adhere with medication (Gupta 2005). Scott and Pope (2002b) found that individuals with bipolar disorders who were non-adherent, were more likely to be living with family members who were significantly less knowledgeable about bipolar disorder and its treatment and showed higher levels of criticism, than the families of adherent subjects. The findings on critical comments confirm the results of an earlier study by Miklowitz *et al.* (1986), which found non-adherence rates to be high in individuals with bipolar disorder living in high expressed emotion environments, particularly if this was also accompanied by a negative affective style of interaction. Perlick *et al.* (2004) reported that family experience of stigma and burden was significantly correlated with high emotional over-involvement and that the latter was associated with higher rates of non-adherence at seven-month follow-up.

Box 8 identifies those factors for which there is consistent evidence of an association with non-adherence or where there are more positive than negative findings of an association.

8

Further Comments on Non-Adherence in Severe Mental Disorders

This section will try to clarify the common themes that apply across schizophrenia and bipolar disorders in terms of the evolution of research on non-adherence as well as the common predictors of adherence. It will also highlight how some predictors (particularly demographic factors) may best be regarded as proxy measures of other underlying mediators or moderators.

Early research on adherence in populations with psychosis or severe mood disorders was overly focused on factors that ultimately identified high risk groups, for example young males. Whereas, clarifying more specific personal attributes, for example holding negative beliefs about the benefits of treatment, would be more sensitive and specific predictors of which individuals from that demographic group may actually become non-adherent, or which individuals from apparently low risk groups, for example an older adult with negative beliefs about treatment, may be destined to become non-adherent. To translate the research findings into clinically meaningful interventions it is important to focus on studies that try to understand the reasons that underlie a decision to stop taking the treatments offered. Indeed, given that clinicians are currently only 50% accurate in their identification of patients who are or are not adherent, it is critical to identify more specific factors for clinicians to explore when they assess the risk of non-adherence in any individual and to disentangle some of the apparently conflicting findings (Scott 2000).

Improving Adherence in Schizophrenia and Bipolar Disorders Mary-Jane Tacchi and Jan Scott

Jamison (1979) and latterly other researchers (e.g. Lingham and Scott 2002; Perlick *et al.* 2004) suggest that, as a first step towards a more systematic approach to predictors, it is useful to consider interacting sets of variables which combine to form the framework for our understanding of non-adherence issues. The frameworks published so far usually comprise 3–6 subgroups of variables clustered together according to common themes, such as:

1. Factors related to the disorder, for example types of symptoms and phase of illness, comorbidity.
2. Treatment issues, for example treatment regime, subjectively reported side effects.
3. Patient factors, for example attitudes to medication and coping style.
4. Clinician-related factors, for example treatment setting, clinicians attitudes to the disorder and its treatment, the clinician's communication style, and their mode of interaction with the patient.
5. Family/environmental factors, for example expressed emotion, attitudes and knowledge about the disorder, level of engagement in treatment process.

A glance at the reviews of schizophrenia and bipolar disorders suggest that rates of non-adherence are similar in both patient populations and that when predictors are clustered together into the above subgroups, there are virtually no differences in the most frequently identified predictors. Indeed, a small scale study by Adams and Scott (2000) of a heterogeneous sample of patients with schizophrenia and severe mood disorders found no significant differences between predictors of adherence when the sample was subdivided according to diagnosis. However, before focusing on how the subgroups noted above can be incorporated into a model to explain the behaviour, it is useful to comment further on patient and clinician factors.

INDIVIDUAL FACTORS

Rather than repeating the factors identified in the sections on schizophrenia and bipolar disorders and listed in Box 7 and Box 8, it may be helpful to reinforce why sociodemographic factors should largely be regarded as unreliable predictors because they may obscure other more useful and valid associations between patient behaviours, beliefs, or personality style and adherence. The aim is not to confuse the reader but simply to highlight that measuring statistical associations between a basic clinical characteristic and adherence will often give contradictory findings, as the research has failed to recognize the need to measure possible underlying causes of the behaviour. The issue will initially be explored using evidence about how living situations and patient age may relate to adherence level. For example, a patient's living situation may actually be positively associated with their adherence level because the support offered by a significant other extends to helping the patient manage their treatment regime, thus obscuring or compensating for the individual's deficits in self-management skills. Alternatively, the negative impact of marital status on adherence in some studies may be explained by research suggesting increased non-adherence in patient's living with relatives demonstrating high levels of expressed emotion, particularly if they verbalize frequent critical comments. It is not the living situation but the different and complex influence of family support and interaction that predicts adherence, which may explain why review papers (e.g. Lacro *et al.* 2002), find no clear evidence for an association between living situation and adherence.

The association between adherence and age is also complex. For example, there is evidence of high rates of non-adherence in those in the early stages of bipolar disorder or being treated for their first episode of psychosis. As the median age of onset of both disorders is below 25 years, an association with age may actually be indicative of early difficulties in adjusting to the disorder and accepting the need for medication. However, there are also several papers suggesting another peak period of non-adherence in individuals with a longer past history of disorder. In some people with a stable mental state, particularly if they have few overt symptoms, the association with lower levels of adherence may indicate that they do not recognize the role of the treatment in keeping them well (as compared with getting them well). Alternatively, the lower level of adherence may be a consequence of a poor clinical response, highlighting a subgroup that is struggling to cope with a poly-pharmacy regime prescribed for treatment refractory symptoms. In this scenario, their non-adherence may be secondary to being unable to cope with multiple dosages, they may have cognitive impairments that impede adherence behaviours, or they may be less adherent because they have lost faith in their treatment and so are ambivalent about taking medication.

A further example of the difficulties of measuring correlations, rather than attempting to target underlying mechanisms, is that the associations reported between adherence and symptom severity or individual symptoms are also variable and, therefore, represent unreliable predictors of non-adherence. The possible exception is insight as this is frequently cited as a risk factor (e.g. Smith *et al.* 1999). However, Rusch and Corrigan (2002) note that there is a problem with the literature about insight because the assessments employed vary considerably and may include measures of some or all of the of the following: adherence-related issues (e.g. perception of need for treatment); symptom-specific elements (e.g. attribution of symptoms to disorder); a time/memory component (e.g. knowledge and awareness about current symptoms and past episodes); and/or cognitive awareness of the disorder. Also, insight may vary over time (even when negative attitudes to treatment do not) and it is a multidimensional construct affected by neuro-cognitive deficits, symptoms of the disorder, and psychological coping mechanisms. There is emerging evidence that components of insight related to the 'denial of severity of illness' or 'impaired illness awareness' may be the critical components of insight that increase the risk of non-adherence across the age spectrum.

With regard to other factors, it is interesting to note that a sensation-seeking personality style was found to be a predictor of non-adherence in schizophrenia and bipolar disorders in a small number of studies where it was measured. Risk-taking behaviour, a characteristic of a sensation-seeking personality, is often associated with increased likelihood of substance misuse. As such the co-occurrence of sensation-seeking personality style, non-adherence, and substance misuse may be partly explained by the fact that non-adherence and substance misuse could both be mediated by a propensity to engage in risk-taking. An alternate explanation is that patients frequently report that they engaged in substance use in an attempt to control their symptoms on their own. Although it may be regarded as a maladaptive coping strategy, it indicates that the patient is trying to cope independently with their problems and might identify a group who may be less likely to accept conventional offers of treatment and support.

Lastly, it is helpful to review the findings on locus of control, a concept referring to the extent to which a person feels that they have control over what happens (internal locus) or that the situation is controlled by other factors (external locus). There is evidence that adherence is more likely if the patient's locus matches the requirements of a situation (Noble 1998). Individuals with an external locus of control are more likely to be adherent with pharmacological interventions for a chronic disorder (McGavock 1996) as beliefs that events are controlled by chance happenings may increase the patients' willingness to take medication as an insurance policy to reduce the risk of relapse (Adams and Scott 2000).

CLINICIAN FACTORS

Specific aspects of the therapeutic alliance will be discussed in detail later in this book. In this section we briefly highlight some of the key themes that recur in the studies of the clinician–patient interaction and its impact on adherence in chronic physical and mental disorders.

There is evidence that doctors overestimate adherence rates in their patients (Lingham and Scott 2002) and in many studies their estimates are no better than chance. Nurses are marginally more accurate (about 60–50% cases correctly classified as adherent or non-adherent). Clinicians also overestimate any agreement with their treatment recommendations by the patient and how these relate to actual patient behaviours (Ley 1982). Pope and Scott (2003) noted that clinicians did not understand patient's reasons for stopping lithium treatment, as the clinicians tended to assume a direct link to illness-related factors, whilst their patients were significantly more likely to endorse beliefs and attitudes about the disorder and what taking medication implied about them as an individual. Such studies suggest a gap in clinician–patient communication and understanding. However, when questioned, clinicians are most likely to identify adherence as a patient-related problem, rather than a behaviour that may be influenced by communication, interaction, or associated with the clinician's actions and reactions (Myers and Midence 1998).

Daltroy *et al.* (1991) provide evidence of the consequences of impaired communication, noting that adherence with medications at four months was 58% when patients reported that they understood the reasons the doctor gave for prescribing it, but only 29% when they did not understand the rationale for the treatment. It is possible that some clinicians give ambivalent messages about the benefits of treatment and of adherence because, despite considerable knowledge about medicine, doctor's adherence to prescribed treatments is no better than that of patients in general (Noble 1998). Furthermore, Coldham *et al.* (2002) identified that 30% of psychiatrists and 65% of non-medical mental health professionals stated that they would not take medication if they were diagnosed as having schizophrenia. If clinicians are ambivalent about treatment it is hardly surprising that patients may also be ambivalent about accepting prescribed medications.

SUMMARY

Important factors influencing adherence across severe mental disorders include the individual's attitudes, beliefs and expectations, their

Box 9 Adherence research in severe mental disorders

1. Early research on factors associated with adherence status was atheoretical and produced unreliable and contradictory findings regarding possible high risk groups.
2. Recent research on adherence and severe mental disorders has taken a more sophisticated approach, attempting to use health belief models to identify the underlying reasons for non-adherence and to explore what combination of variables explain individual adherence behaviour.

views of the disorder, individual coping strategies, and the attitudes and beliefs of others (family and clinicians). The behaviour is probably further modified by factors such as the ability to manage a complex treatment regime and subjective experience of side effects. These elements can be incorporated into a coherent model of health beliefs such as that employed in general medicine. A number of different theories have evolved to explain an individual's response to chronic physical disorders such as diabetes mellitus, hypertension and renal diseases, and to explain engagement or non-engagement with treatment. These models have only recently been applied to severe mental disorders (Fenton *et al.* 1997; Scott 2000) because for too long psychiatry research employed simplistic approaches to adherence and focused on patient demographics and medication side effects. Studies employing measures that look at underlying mechanisms to explain the relationship between patient beliefs and adherence behaviour are now emerging, and suggest patients with severe mental disorders are more similar than different to those with severe physical disorders with regard to their health belief models (Box 9). We will therefore describe one health belief model to give an example of how these theories can be used to provide a systematic approach to exploring adherence behaviour.

9

Model for Conceptualizing Adherence Behaviour

The 'Cognitive Representation of Illness' model (Leventhal *et al.* 1992) describes how an individual constructs an internal representation of what is happening to them when they experience physical or psychological symptoms and how they react to this scenario. It is an example of a self-regulatory model and so it is particularly useful in the current climate of mental health services, as a self-regulation theory assumes an individual tries to be an active problem-solver and that their behaviours represent their personal effort to resolve the problem caused by a health 'threat'. Horne and Weinman (1995) suggest the individual's coping strategies represent an attempt to 'close the gap' between their current health status and their desired future state. The cognitive representation of illness model has three core elements:

1. A cognitive representation, which reflects the meaning of the health threat to the individual. This can be activated by internal (symptoms) or external (information in the media) cues.
2. An action plan, which is the coping strategy developed and instigated by the individual to deal with the threat.
3. The individual's appraisal of the outcome of the coping strategy.

It is suggested that, no matter what the nature of the symptoms, most individuals organize their thinking about any health threat around five key themes (Scott and Tacchi 2002). These are: What is it (identity)? Why has it happened (cause)? How long will it last, will it recur (timeline)? What effects will it have (consequences)? What can

Improving Adherence in Schizophrenia and Bipolar Disorders Mary-Jane Tacchi and Jan Scott

I do to make it go away (cure/control)? Thus, the structure of the representation is a stable aspect of the model but the content of the cognitive representations may be idiosyncratic and can be influenced by past experiences or the views of significant others.

The second component of the model suggests that if symptoms occur, individuals will make some attempt to cope with them. Crucially, their choice of a particular coping strategy to cure or control the problem (e.g. taking medication or not) will be influenced by whether that seems to be a logical step given their ideas about the perceived identity, cause, timeline, controllability, and consequences of the symptoms they have experienced. Taking medication or indeed seeking professional help may be one of a number of coping behaviours employed by the individual.

The individual will next appraise their coping strategy and come to a decision about how effective it has been. They will then continue to use or modify this coping strategy accordingly. If the many alternative coping strategies are all ineffective the individual may reappraise their cognitive representation, and then institute a further sequence of actions based on the new view they adopt. Finally, the model suggests that individuals who perceive coherence between their concrete experiences of the symptoms, the meaning they have attached to them, and the explanation offered to them by a significant other (this may be a health professional) are more likely to engage with health services or adhere with the interventions that are suggested. This is predictable as the coherence between the patients' view and the external feedback mean that any suggested course of action (such as a programme of treatment) appears logical.

The model is not universally accepted and some criticisms have been made about the notion that emotional and cognitive processes occur in parallel. This aspect of the model explains a common observation that some individuals do not seek treatment even if they perceive their health problem as a significant threat. However, classic cognitive models would postulate a direct link between emotions and cognitions and regard health beliefs as a reflection of other underlying beliefs and assumptions related to views of the self, world, and future (Scott 1999). Despite these criticisms, a core strength of the model is that it sees the individual's cognitive representation and coping strategies as a dynamic process evolving over time. Furthermore, it identifies the individual's pattern of behaviour as being 'logical' in that it makes sense to them as the problem-solving strategies employed are a direct result of the attributions and evaluation of the problem. For this reason, the model is sometimes referred to as a 'common sense' model and non-adherence may be viewed as 'intelligent non-adherence' because this behaviour is entirely consistent with the patient's perceptions about the identity and causes of the problem and what would be an effective strategy to control the threat.

As can be seen in Box 10, the elements of the model can be drawn into a flow diagram that shows how all these factors may be associated with adherence behaviour. Furthermore, we have incorporated a number of other issues that may influence an individual's decision-making (Scott and Tacchi 2002). For example, when reviewing the identity and consequences of the disorder, individuals will appraise the threat posed by their symptoms. If they perceive that the disorder represents a severe threat to their well-being or see themselves as particularly susceptible to relapses, they may be more inclined to accept medication (see Adams and Scott 2000). Similarly, when considering whether the

Box 10 A flow diagram of factors influencing likelihood of adherence

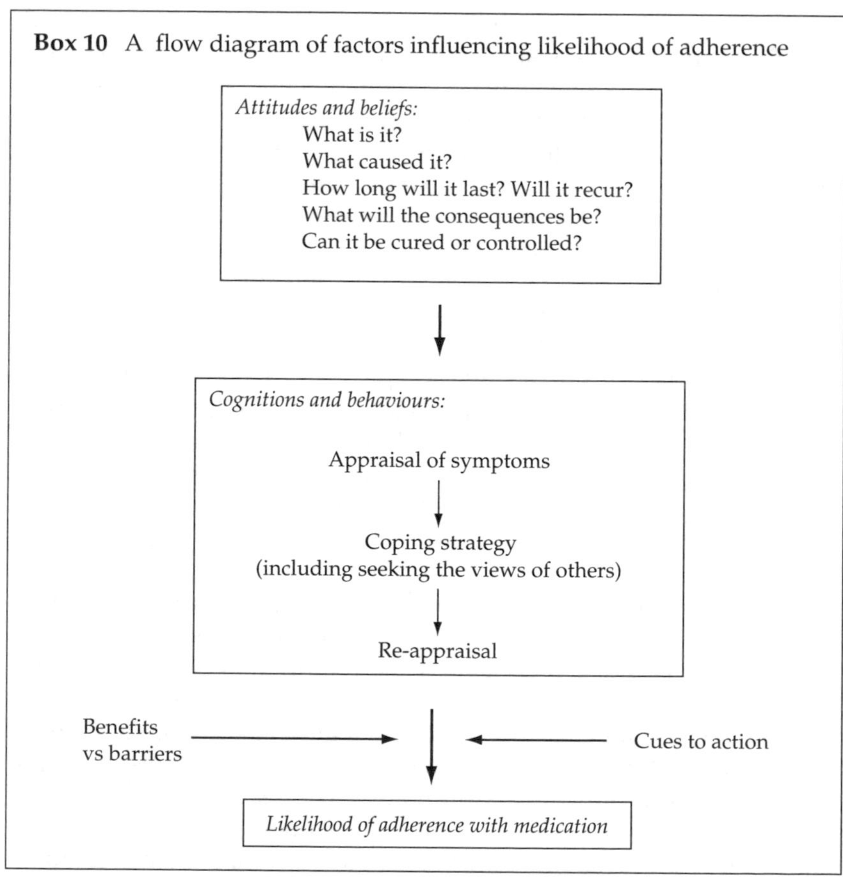

problem can be cured or controlled, the individual will assess the relative benefits of taking medication versus the potential barriers to such adherence (e.g. improved sleep versus personally upsetting side effects such as weight gain). Also, an individual may be prompted to re-engage with treatment because of early symptoms of relapse (internal cue) or to stop treatment because of a negative article in the media about, for example, the risk of becoming dependent on drugs if they take the prescribed medications (external cue). The model outlined also offers the possibility for intervening at different points to bring about a change in behaviour.

Part Two

10

Interventions to Enhance Adherence—Research Evidence

Despite the growing acceptance that medication non-adherence is a significant public health issue associated with financial, social, and illness costs, there is a limited evidence base on the use of specific interventions to target the problem. The available literature describes interventions of various types that have been utilized in schizophrenia and bipolar disorders. Some studies have specifically measured medication adherence as a primary outcome (primary outcome studies). Whereas, others described psychosocial interventions that were not used purely to address medication non-adherence, but have reported the effect of the intervention on adherence as a secondary outcome measure or an incidental finding (secondary outcome studies). Obviously, the former provide more robust evidence; however, given the lack of research on the topic, both types of study will be reviewed to give as much information as possible for translation into clinical practice.

The studies on schizophrenia and bipolar disorders will be reviewed separately. At the end of each review the key findings are summarized. Finally, some interventions that have been successful in depression are reviewed, as this research may be relevant to bipolar depression.

Improving Adherence in Schizophrenia and Bipolar Disorders Mary-Jane Tacchi and Jan Scott

11

Schizophrenia

PRIMARY OUTCOME STUDIES

Psychoeducation

'Psychoeducation' is a commonly used term but there is little agreement on what the term actually means. There is a general acknowledgement that it aims to increase a patient's knowledge and understanding of disorder (Pekkala and Merinder 2002), and it is assumed that this enables a person with schizophrenia to cope more effectively with the disorder. Psychoeducation may be defined as the education for a person with mental disorder in subject areas that serve the goals of treatment and rehabilitation, and it usually involves interaction between the information giver and the patient. Education can take various forms, for example one-to-one or small group teaching, and can involve the use of written material, didactic lectures, videotapes, or a combination of these approaches. Education is usually a gradual process by which a person gains knowledge through learning. However, this is where the boundaries between psychoeducation and other interventions may become blurred as many researchers (e.g. Rankin and Stallings 1996) suggest that learning involves more than acquiring knowledge and can involve cognitive, affective, and psychomotor processes, whilst Falvo (1994) stated that learning implies changes in behaviour, skills, and/or attitudes.

Studies of psychoeducation in schizophrenia use a range of interventions, but the majority focus primarily on dissemination of knowledge about schizophrenia and treatment options to achieve medication adherence without focusing on attitudinal and behavioural change. Studies have provided education to individuals, to groups, and to relatives of patients. The interaction between information giver and

Improving Adherence in Schizophrenia and Bipolar Disorders Mary-Jane Tacchi and Jan Scott

patient is stressed and programmes tend to address the disorder from a multidimensional viewpoint including familial, social, biological, and pharmacological perspectives. In addition patients are provided with varying amounts of support, information, and management strategies.

A Cochrane Database systematic review (Pekkala and Merinder 2002) examined ten randomized controlled trials of psychoeducation in schizophrenia, and five of these studies were included in an earlier systematic review of seven randomized controlled trials on the same topic (Merinder 2000). Results showed that only one intervention led to improved adherence (Bauml *et al.* 1996). One hundred and sixty-three subjects were randomly allocated to a control treatment or to a group intervention providing verbal and written information delivered over eight sessions. In one year there was a significant advantage for the intervention group as demonstrated on a continuous measure of adherence (1–4 with a low score indicating greater adherence) with this group showing a mean adherence rating of 1.7 compared to 2.1 in the control group (Weighted Mean Difference –0.4; 95% Confidence Intervals –0.6 to –0.2).

Interventions that did not report improved adherence included an individual educational session (MacPherson *et al.* 1996) and individual counselling sessions by a hospital pharmacist in the presence of a key relative (Razali *et al.* 1995). Group interventions that did not report improved adherence included a medication management group (Goulet *et al.* 1993), an education group providing information and problem-solving skills (Atkinson *et al.* 1996), and an eight-session educational intervention including information giving and discussion (Merinder 1999). Goldman and Quinn (1988) and Streicker *et al.* (1986) reported that extended courses of group psychoeducation (35–75 sessions) did not significantly change adherence levels.

A further review by Dolder *et al.* (2003) showed that only one of four educational interventions improved adherence. Seltzer *et al.* (1980) described a cohort study of 67 inpatients with schizophrenia (44), bipolar disorder (16), and unipolar depression (7). They were allocated to a control group or to a psychoeducation programme consisting of nine lectures about their disorder and its pharmacological treatment, combined with behavioural reinforcement for desirable medication routines. Given the inclusion of the latter approach, Zygmunt *et al.* (2002) suggested that this was not therefore a purely educational intervention as it contained elements of behaviour modification. Group resources were also used to help patients deal with fears and resistance that interfere with adherence, and patients were provided with a drug datasheet upon discharge. At follow-up at five months, non-adherence was monitored by urine tests and pill counts and it was found that the intervention group showed a non-adherence rate of 6% according to urine test and 9% according to pill counts, whereas the control group had a rate of 25% and 66%, respectively. The study has been criticized because of a substantial dropout rate both in the intervention group and in the comparison group, which has raised concerns about possible attrition bias.

Brown *et al.* (1987) randomly assigned 30 patients to receive one of four interventions: verbal information about their medication but not about side effects; verbal and written information about their medication but not side effects; verbal information about medication and side effects; or verbal and written information about medication and side effects. Results showed that although patients' knowledge about their medication improved with the interventions, this failed to translate into any change in adherence. However, it must be borne in mind that the small sample size may have led to false negative results.

A number of studies have utilized family psychoeducation interventions. However, the trial by Xiang *et al.* (1994), which investigated family therapy in a rural province in China, is one of the few demonstrating significant benefits from this approach. The intervention group ($n = 36$) received a teaching programme designed to provide family members with a basic knowledge of mental disorders and their treatment. The aim was to allow family members to understand the patient and their disorder and to understand how to look after the patient physically and psychologically. The intervention helped family members identify and solve problems and to improve their knowledge of mental health rehabilitation. This was achieved using family visits, workshops, and monthly supervision. The comparison group ($n = 36$) were provided with usual treatment only. At four months the rates of full adherence (patients were receiving a depot injection) were significantly improved in the intervention group [47%] versus the control group [15%], and the rates of full and partial adherence combined were 75% and 34% in the intervention and control groups, respectively. However, other studies utilizing psychoeducation and family interventions failed to demonstrate an improvement in medication adherence (e.g. Leff *et al.* 1990; Zhang *et al.* 1994), as did an inpatient family intervention (Haas *et al.* 1988) and a family relapse prevention programme (Herz 1996).

Outcomes for psychoeducation suggest that the benefits of such interventions nearly always include knowledge acquisition. However, knowledge alone does not appear to lead to a change in adherence behaviour. Didactic approaches to psychoeducation produced marginal, non-significant improvements in adherence levels, but up to 50% of these studies show some improvements in clinical outcomes (Zygmunt *et al.* 2002). The improvements in adherence level for combined educational and behavioural interventions are higher, but there is no evidence about the most effective length of a course (Dolder *et al.* 2003).

Behavioural and Cognitive Behavioural Interventions

Behavioural Interventions

Behavioural interventions assume that behaviours are acquired through learning and conditioning and can be modified by targeting, shaping, rewarding, or reinforcing specific behavioural patterns. Interventions include skill building, practising activities, behavioural modelling, and reinforcement strategies.

A number of studies have shown behavioural interventions to be successful in improving medication adherence. Boczkowski *et al.* (1995) randomly assigned 36 males with schizophrenia to behavioural training, didactic psychoeducation or standard treatment. The behavioural intervention consisted of patients being told the importance of adhering to medication and each participant was helped to tailor the prescribed regime so that it was better adapted to their personal habits and routines. This involved identifying a highly visible location for placement of medications and pairing the daily medication intake with specific routine behaviours. Each participant was given a self-monitoring spiral calendar that featured a dated slip of paper for each dose of medication. The participant was instructed to keep the calendar near their medications and to tear off a slip each time they took a pill. At a three-month follow-up, there was a significant improvement in the behavioural intervention group compared with the other two groups. Eight out of eleven patients who had received behavioural therapy showed adherence with 80% or more of their medication, whereas only three out of eleven in the psychoeducation intervention group showed such levels. However, as highlighted by Gray *et al.* (2002) it is important to note that whilst adherence as measured by pill count was significantly improved, patient- and observer-reported adherence did not improve. This suggests that self-report either was inaccurate or raises the possibility that patients had learned to adjust the number of tablets returned for the purpose of pill counting to falsely demonstrate improved adherence.

Cramer and Rosenheck (1999) described a randomized controlled trial of 60 patients allocated to usual treatment or to the MUSE (Medication Usage Skills for Effectiveness) programme that teaches simple techniques of how to remember daily medication doses to patients with severe mental disorders. The intervention consisted of an initial session of 15 minutes where the patient was taught to develop cues to remember the dose times. The intervention utilized electronic monitoring pill bottles with special caps that display the date and time of each bottle opening. Patients were also taught to check the dose cap to see when their next dose of medication was due. Five-minute meetings were held each month at which the patient was provided with visual feedback in the form of a calendar showing the number of times the bottle had been opened and when. The control group received several minutes of general instructions about the importance of taking medication. Results showed significant improvement in the intervention group. The mean one-month adherence rate was 81% in the intervention group and 68% in the control group, at six months the rate was 76% and 57%, respectively. This preliminary data appears to demonstrate the potential application of a simple focused intervention to enhance adherence behaviour.

Eckman *et al.* (1990) investigated a behavioural programme in improving adherence and medication management skills in 160 outpatients with schizophrenia. Patients followed a structured module in groups for about 3 hours per week over four months. The multimedia module used videotaped demonstrations, focused instruction, specialized role play, video feedback, and practice in the real world to focus on four skill areas: information regarding the benefits of antipsychotic medication, correct self-administration, evaluation of medication effects, and identifying side effects and negotiating medication issues with health care providers. Adherence improved significantly from about 60% pre-intervention to 80% post-intervention. However, it can be argued that this group had a high baseline adherence rate before intervention and were therefore more likely to participate in research, and may not be typical of those at high risk of non-adherence.

Razali *et al.* (2000) studied the effectiveness of culturally modified behavioural family therapy compared with a standard version of behavioural family therapy in 166 individuals. Post-randomization, there were 74 subjects in the culturally modified intervention group and 69 in the behavioural family therapy group. Culturally modified therapy provided an explanation of the concept of schizophrenia with respect to the prevailing cultural beliefs concerning mental disorders (which in Malaysia included ideas about the role of the supernatural). It also gave a rationale for various treatments, allowed the counsellor to provide a positive attitude towards modern treatment, and provided clear instructions about dose, frequency and side effects of medications, and reminders of follow-up appointments. Adherence was measured globally as a percentage of the total prescribed dosages actually taken during the previous six months. At follow-up, 73% in the group receiving culturally modified therapy as compared to 59% in the control group were adherent with 90% of their prescribed medication. At one year, rates were 85% and 55% respectively. Interestingly, the trial by Telles *et al.* (1995) failed to show improvement in medication adherence at 12 months for a behavioural management family intervention as compared to case management in a sample of 40 immigrant families. Perhaps this is an indication that taking cultural contexts and models into account is critical to the success of these family interventions.

Cognitive Behavioural Interventions

Lecompte and Pelc (1996) tested a cognitive behavioural programme targeted at changing adherence patterns through the use of five therapeutic strategies: engagement, psychoeducation, identifying prodromal symptoms, developing coping strategies and behavioural strategies for reinforcing adherence behaviour, and correcting false beliefs about medication. Sixty-four non-adherent psychotic patients were randomly assigned to receive either the active intervention or a control treatment of unstructured conversation. Surprisingly, the primary outcome measure was the duration of hospitalization one year before and one year after the intervention, which the authors argued was a useful indirect measure of adherence. Patients receiving the cognitive behavioural intervention spent significantly less time in hospital in the year after as compared to the year before the intervention, but no significant difference was reported than those in the control group. Although these findings suggest the intervention is beneficial, it is not certain that this improvement can be attributed solely to improved adherence, which obviously undermines the impact of the study.

Motivational Interviewing

Motivational interviewing is an intervention that was originally designed to help people identify the costs and benefits related to their personal goals as well as the advantages and disadvantages of services that help people achieve these goals (Miller and Rollnick 1991). Motivational interviewing is applied to a broad range of problems in chronic illness management and substance misuse. It can be defined as 'a directive client centred counselling style for eliciting behaviour change by helping clients to explore and resolve ambivalence' (Rollnick and Miller 1995). Although behavioural analysis is used, motivational interviewing does not try to force the person into accepting the evidence of advantages of a new behaviour but considers the value of letting persons carefully discover advantages and disadvantages of their behaviour for themselves.

Corrigan *et al.* (2001) suggest that motivational interviewing can be applied in schizophrenia to improve medication adherence but certain modifications have to be made to combat the presence of negative symptoms or lack of motivation. Hayward *et al.* (1995) used an intervention of medication self-management based on motivational interviewing which aimed to allow patients and clinicians to work collaboratively to examine medication issues. Twenty-one inpatients received three 30-minute sessions of either medication self-management or non-directive discussion on any issue except medication. The pilot work showed trends in favour of the intervention group with regard to adherence and attitudes towards treatment but none reached statistical significance. This led to the development of the longer, more structured intervention 'Compliance Therapy' (Kemp *et al.* 1996), which modified motivational interviewing techniques to give particular attention to the therapeutic relationship and to make the approach useful with patients suffering from psychosis and combined this with cognitive behavioural techniques (see below).

Compliance Therapy

'Compliance therapy' utilizes motivational interviewing and cognitive behavioural approaches. The therapy is described in detail in the treatment manual (Kemp *et al.* 1997). The key techniques are those of reflective listening, regular summarizing, inductive questioning, exploring ambivalence, developing discrepancy between present behaviour and broader goals, and using normalizing rationales. Kemp *et al.* (1998) reported a randomized controlled trial of 74 patients with psychosis allocated to 4–6 sessions of compliance therapy versus 4–6 sessions of supportive counselling. Results demonstrated a significant effect upon adherence in the intervention group as compared to the control group immediately post treatment and at an 18-month follow-up. Results equated to a mean difference in adherence of 19% between the two groups, which represented a clinically meaningful difference of 1–2 points on the observer-rated seven-point scale (where 1 = complete refusal to take medication and 7 = active participation in treatment and takes responsibility for regimen). However, O'Donnell *et al.* (2003) failed to replicate Kemp's findings on the utility of compliance therapy in a one-year study of 56 inpatients with schizophrenia. The study did show that attitudes to treatment at baseline predicted adherence at one year, thus suggesting early identification of attitudes towards medication may be useful in clinical practice.

The different forms of behavioural and cognitive behavioural therapies show that these approaches, in individual or group format, can improve medication adherence. The interventions that most frequently lead to improved adherence are those that: (a) target the therapeutic relationship (motivational interviewing and compliance therapy); (b) have some method of exploring the patient's model of their disorder including their attitudes, beliefs and expectations as well as presenting the clinician's views of the disorder and its treatment; and (c) employ concrete problem-solving strategies and specific instructions such as reminders and reinforcement techniques, self-monitoring tools and a written treatment plan.

Multi-Modal Approaches

Kelly and Scott (1990) describe a study of 418 patients with schizophrenia or other psychotic disorders. Patients were assigned to one of three intervention groups or to a control group receiving standard treatment alone. The first intervention group received a series of up to three home visits focused on assessing the patient's current level of adherence, devising an appropriate behavioural approach for improving it, and encouraging a positive and supportive environment. The core of the intervention was the development of an individual 'compliance plan'. The second intervention—a clinic visit—was aimed at improving patient-provider communications designed to teach the patient to become an active health care consumer. The third active intervention was both the clinic and the home visits. Two hundred and seventy-three patients [65%] completed follow-up at six months and ratings at this point demonstrated that adherence was significantly improved among the experimental groups compared with the control group. Continuous levels of adherence with medication in the week prior to assessment at baseline and at six months were reported as: home visit group, 54% vs 73%; clinic group, 45% vs 65%; combined group, 56% vs 66%; and 58% vs 88% in the control group. This difference in adherence between active treatments and the control treatment was statistically significant.

Azrin and Teichner (1998) randomly assigned 39 patients (schizophrenia = 21; bipolar disorders = 10; and unipolar disorder = 8) to a behavioural intervention delivered to individual patients ($n = 13$) or to patients and their family ($n = 13$) and compared this with a control treatment (receiving information pack describing psychotropic medications). The two intervention groups were taught detailed behavioural guidelines for each step of the medication-taking sequence. In the combined approach, family members collaborated with patients in implementing these behavioural strategies. Results were reported as the change in pre- and post-intervention adherence rates as assessed by pill counts. The change in adherence rate was 19% (pre = 76% vs post=95%) in the family group, 22% (70% vs 92%) in the individual group but only 9% (73% vs 64%) in the control group, that is, the intervention groups showed significantly greater adherence than the comparison group, but the active treatments were not significantly different from each other. Interestingly, no improvements in clinical symptoms were reported in any group.

Guimon *et al.* (1993) studied a patient-and-family approach that involved group discussion of medication attitudes and behaviours. During group sessions patients discussed their conflicts about taking medication while a therapist and other group members provided suggestions about how to address these conflicts. Family members participated in similar groups. The intervention group showed superior medication adherence compared with standard care at 3- and 12-month follow-up.

Multimodal approaches, by definition, recognize that educational, behavioural, and affective strategies are likely to improve adherence. There is a trend for studies that employ a specific and clear rationale for the intervention used to be effective whether the course of therapy is of long or short duration. It appears that individual, group and family work can all be undertaken using multimodal approaches.

SECONDARY OUTCOME STUDIES

The following studies have reported levels of medication adherence but were not specifically targeting this behaviour. This reduces the weight that can be given to the results; however, these studies provide useful information for clinical practice.

Psychoeducation

Falloon *et al.* (1985) described a family-based approach to enhance the problem-solving capacity of the patient and their family care givers compared with an individual patient-orientated approach of similar intensity over a two-year period. The family group focused on family problem solving with less attention to patient-related issues and utilized structured education of the entire family unit about schizophrenia and its management using home-based sessions. A number of outcomes were reported. With regard to medication adherence, the family intervention succeeded in minimizing non-adherence (family intervention rate=20% vs individual therapy rate=50%) and patients receiving family therapy group were also less likely to transfer on to depot medications (Zygmunt *et al.* 2002). However, there was no evidence that the effects of family therapy were mediated only by increased adherence.

Smith *et al.* (1992) evaluated a group educational intervention based on material developed for family psychoeducation. The intervention was provided to small groups and the concept of schizophrenia, symptoms, and treatment were discussed in four fortnightly sessions. A booklet was given to reinforce the information presented in the groups. Twenty-eight patients were divided into two groups according to the presence or absence of positive symptoms. Both groups received the same educational intervention. The researchers observed that although significant improvements in knowledge were found in both groups, patients who had no residual symptoms gained more information than those who were still symptomatic, but neither group showed any improvement in adherence level.

Behavioural and Cognitive Behavioural Interventions

Tarrier *et al.* (1988) compared two different types of behavioural intervention with an education only group versus routine treatment in 48 subjects with schizophrenia. The primary goal of the interventions was to reduce relapse rates. The education group received a two session educational programme designed to give patients and relatives extensive information about schizophrenia and how to manage it in the home environment. The behavioural interventions were both of nine-month duration and of similar content. The families initially received the education programme followed by stress management, goal setting, and training in procedures to achieve these goals. Both behavioural interventions were didactic in that families were taught skills with which to manage schizophrenia. Patients with a relative expressing high expressed emotion (EE) were allocated to all four interventions, whilst patients with low EE relatives were assigned to education only or to routine treatment. Results showed that medication adherence was achieved by 68% of all patients with no significant differences between the groups.

Multi-Modal Approaches

Hogarty *et al.* (1991) undertook a two-year follow-up of patients from high EE environments who had been randomly assigned to one of four treatment cells: (1) family psychoeducation: (2) social skills training: (3) both: or (4) supportive therapy plus medication. Family treatment involved an education and management strategy intended to lower the emotional climate of the home through formal education about the disorder and strategies to encourage family members to become allies in the treatment process. Social skills training employed behavioural techniques of modelling instruction, role play and feedback, and assigned homework assignments. It was found that medication non-adherence was reduced significantly in the experimental conditions (rate=21%) compared with the control group (rate=40%).

Velligan *et al.* (2000) described a randomized control trial of cognitive adaptation training in 45 patients with schizophrenia. Cognitive adaptation training (CAT) is a manual-driven intervention employing a series of compensatory strategies based on neuropsychological, behavioural, and occupational therapy principles. Training includes a comprehensive behavioural assessment to quantify the level of apathy and disinhibited behaviour, and a neuropsychological assessment to examine the level of executive functioning, attention, and memory. Patients were randomly assigned to one of three treatment conditions: (1) standard medication follow-up; (2) standard medication follow-up plus cognitive adaptation training; and (3) standard follow-up plus a condition that controlled for therapist contact time and for changes in the patient's environment. Patients received weekly therapy over a nine-month period. The mean between group differences in positive symptom scores was significant, with improvement in symptoms in the CAT group and worsening in the other two groups, and the CAT group also experienced significantly fewer relapses. There were no differences in negative symptom scores between the groups. When the level of functioning was examined this was significantly improved in the intervention group. Although medication adherence was not a primary outcome measure, the authors allude to the possibility that differences in rates of medication adherence between the groups could explain some of the differences in clinical and social outcomes.

Service Responses

Different models of community-based care have been developed to meet the diverse needs of those with severe mental disorders. The key components of such interventions are the provision of a strong and supportive social network, close monitoring of clinical status including the medication regime, provision of stable housing, and other supportive services (Marshall and Lockwood 2002). Zygmunt *et al.* (2002) noted that four of the ten community studies reviewed reported that the intervention was associated with significantly greater medication adherence. Although few of the studies included a rigorous assessment of medication adherence and only half provided specific information on their method for measuring adherence, we give a brief overview of some of the interventions that were associated with enhanced medication adherence.

Assertive Community Treatment

Stein and Test (1980) describe a conceptual model of community treatment that encompasses six areas. These are material resources, coping skills to meet the demands of community life, motivation to persevere and remain involved with life, freedom from pathologically dependent relationships, support and education of community members who are involved with patients, and a support system that assertively helps patients with the previous requirements. They describe implementation of this programme, which they entitled 'Training in Community Living', and compared this with short-term hospitalization plus after care. The study reports many outcomes but at 8- and 12-month follow-ups adherence with antipsychotic medication in the experimental group was significantly improved compared with the control group. Following the intervention when patients returned to traditional community programmes these benefits were lost. Bush *et al.* (1990) compared assertive community treatment versus standard case management and showed improvement in medication adherence at 24 months. Likewise, Ford *et al.* (1995) compared intensive case management with standard case management and also showed improvement in medication adherence at 18 months. However, other studies of enhanced care management versus standard care have failed to show improvement, for example Bond *et al.* (1988), compared assertive community treatment with standard case management and at six months there was no difference in adherence between the groups. Modrcin *et al.* (1988) compared 'strengths case management' versus standard case management and showed no difference in adherence between the two groups at four months. Similarly, Solomon and Draine (1995) compared intensive consumer case management with intensive case management and showed no difference in medication adherence between the two groups at two years.

Dixon *et al.* (1997) noted that despite the uneven quality of research into the effects of community care programmes on medication adherence, many programmes closely monitor patients with a history of non-adherence and consider regular medication use as an important treatment goal. It is suggested that the reduction in hospitalization associated with such models of care may in part be a consequence of improved medication adherence.

Supported Housing Projects

A cross-sectional naturalistic survey by Grunebaum *et al.* (2001) of adults with schizophrenia living in supportive housing facilities in New York City, showed that direct supervision of medication was associated with better adherence. A structured interview was used to assess medication adherence, degree of medication supervision, opinions about medication, and regime complexity. The main finding was that medication supervision was related to the duration of medication non-adherence. The data suggested that medication supervision is more important than medication type or regime complexity in determining medication adherence within residential facilities. Previous studies have shown that supervision of medication by family members or friends is associated with better adherence (Fenton *et al.* 1997) but persons living in supportive housing are often without significant others to supervise their treatment. The results of this pilot study suggest that residential staff could take over this function and improve adherence by supervising medication administration.

It is noteworthy that service-based interventions implicitly target the issue of engaging the patient with their key worker or developing a strong link to a support service such as day care or supported housing. Having established a working alliance, many of the other interventions used in these programmes incorporate problem-solving and behavioural strategies noted to be useful in promoting adherence in the primary outcome studies. Therefore, it is not surprising that about 50% of studies of service-based approaches to the care and treatment of severe mental disorders also report a significant improvement in medication adherence (Zygmunt *et al.* 2002).

SUMMARY OF FINDINGS IN SCHIZOPHRENIA

Zygmunt *et al.* (2002) reviewed 39 studies that aimed to improve adherence in schizophrenia. They reported that 33% of those studies reported significant intervention effects, but that studies specifically targeting adherence (primary outcome studies) reported greater benefits than more broadly based approaches (secondary outcome studies), with improvements in adherence rates of 55% compared with 26%. The majority of studies reporting improved adherence [69%] also reported improved clinical outcomes.

This review concurs with Roter *et al.* (2000) who concluded from a meta-analysis of interventions to improve adherence in other chronic disease states that comprehensive interventions combining educational, behavioural and/or affective components are more effective than single focused interventions. Educational and behavioural strategies are well described elsewhere. Affective strategies are described as those that have attempted to influence medication adherence through appeals to feelings and emotions or social relationships and social supports (Dolder *et al.* 2003). Thus studies such as those by Rizali *et al.* (2000), Falloon *et al.* (1985) and Dixon *et al.* (1997) would be regarded as having a significant affective component.

The evidence from primary and secondary studies shows that purely didactic psychoeducation interventions are the least effective for improving medication adherence (Merinder 2000). Those interventions that employ educational and behavioural strategies are more likely to be successful. Individual and group approaches utilizing these strategies produce significant improvements in adherence, with or without changes in knowledge about the disorder. Successful interventions that improve both knowledge and adherence are often highly focused on a particular model (e.g. compliance therapy, behaviour and education group). If a generic approach is employed, the therapy needs to be longer in duration to produce a significant impact, and it is estimated that about 6–8 sessions is required as a minimum. The quality of the educational programme and therapy delivered to patients is a strong predictor of gains in knowledge and adherence (Mullen *et al.* 1985). Interestingly, patient characteristics (age, gender, duration of illness) do not appear to reliably predict response to the intervention, although there is some evidence of a dose-response effect on insight, where individuals with a long history of schizophrenia benefit from a more prolonged intervention (MacPherson *et al.* 1996).

Interventions can also be subdivided according to the format such as individual, group, family interventions or service-based approaches.

Box 11 Summary of interventions in schizophrenia

Intervention (number of studies)	Improved knowledge	Improved adherence	Improved outcomes
Didactic psychoeducation (n = 7)	85%	14%	14%
Psychoeducation plus behavioural interventions (n = 11)	83%	75%	45%
Behavioural and cognitive behavioural interventions (n = 5)	100%	80%	60%
Multi-modal interventions (n = 12)	75%	75%	50%
Service-based responses (n = 10)	Not known	40%	50%

The most significant finding when studies are assessed in this way is that family interventions are *less* effective than other formats *unless* this also incorporates significant behavioural elements (Zygmunt *et al.* 2002). Multimodal approaches, including different types and formats of intervention, are generally helpful across a range of problem areas, but it is difficult to isolate any active ingredients that may specifically enhance adherence.

As shown in Box 11, interventions utilizing combined strategies are more effective in increasing adherence. These approaches often show gains beyond increased knowledge and insight, such as decreased relapse or hospitalization rates, and increased social functioning.

12

Bipolar Disorder

There are considerably fewer studies in bipolar disorders of interventions that may increase medication adherence. There is only one published small-scale randomized controlled trial specifically assessing this issue. Likewise, psychological therapies are less well developed for bipolar disorders than for schizophrenia. For this reason, the section on secondary outcome studies will simply give an overview of the state of research on these therapies and highlight the publications that may indicate an effect on adherence.

PRIMARY OUTCOME STUDIES

Psychoeducation

Harvey and Peet (1991) explored the effect on lithium adherence in 60 clinic attendees allocated to a brief educational programme or to usual treatment. The intervention consisted of a simple 12-minute videotaped lecture with graphic illustrations of how lithium is used to treat affective disorder. This was complimented with an illustrated transcript. Patients then received a visit two weeks later to discuss any particular difficulties they were having with lithium. Medication adherence was measured by self-reporting of missed doses, serum lithium levels, and serum RBC lithium levels. Compared to usual treatment, the education group showed a reduction in their self-reported missed doses of lithium in the six weeks after the intervention (this just failed to reach statistical significance, $p=0.07$). There were no significant between-group differences in plasma and RBC lithium levels.

Improving Adherence in Schizophrenia and Bipolar Disorders Mary-Jane Tacchi and Jan Scott

Behavioural and Cognitive Behavioural Interventions

Cochran (1984) described the effect of a modified cognitive behavioural therapy intervention aimed at altering cognitions and behaviours that interfere with adherence with lithium. Twenty-eight new referrals to a lithium clinic were randomized to the intervention, which consisted of one hour a week for six weeks and was based on Beck *et al.*'s (1979) model, or to usual treatment. Adherence was measured using self-report, informant report, physician report, serum lithium levels, and a 'compliance index'. The latter was a composite measure of medication consumption, attendance at appointments, and serum lithium levels. Results showed that immediately post treatment and at a six-month follow-up, patients in the intervention group when compared with standard care patients were significantly more adherent according to the 'compliance index' and by physicians ratings, although there was no significant differences in self- or informant-reported compliance or serum lithium levels. Patients receiving cognitive behaviour therapy were also significantly less likely than those in the control group to terminate lithium treatment against medical advice (21% vs 57%) or be hospitalized. Given the brevity of the intervention, the results suggest that this is potentially a highly cost-effective intervention. However, the small sample size and lack of any replication undermines this claim.

A pilot study of cognitive concordance therapy in 10 outpatients with bipolar disorder who were non-adherent with lithium prophylaxis showed improvement in lithium adherence following a six-session intervention (Scott and Tacchi 2002). The intervention utilized a health belief model to allow the clinician and patients to reach a collaborative understanding of the disorder, its treatment, and each other's aims and goals. Specific behavioural and cognitive interventions were then employed to effect change in adherence behaviour. The emphasis was on the collaborative nature of the therapeutic alliance, which allowed open and honest discussion, and realistic appraisal of progress. Pre- and post-intervention assessments demonstrated statistically significant improvements in attitudes towards lithium, self-reported lithium adherence and serum lithium levels (mean levels increased from 0.41 mmol/L at baseline to 0.60 mmol/L at six-month follow-up). This approach is now the subject of a further study.

Other Interventions

A number of early publications on the use of group therapies in bipolar disorders advocated their role in enhancing medication adherence. In many studies it is not clear that this was the primary focus of the intervention and few therapies were compared with other treatment interventions in controlled treatment trials. However, there were some encouraging results that may be of some relevance to day-to-day clinical practice. As such we give details of one study as an example of these approaches. Shakir *et al.* (1979) described the effects of group interpersonal therapy on lithium adherence and course of bipolar disorder in a small cohort of patients. The group consisted of 15 individuals with bipolar disorder, 10 of who had histories of poor adherence to lithium prophylaxis. The group comprised 8–10 adults who met weekly for 75 minutes; the average duration of treatment was about one year. Group members were free to discuss specific problems or concerns regarding lithium treatment at any time. The authors reported that initially patients were sceptical of both the long-term efficacy of lithium prophylaxis and the benefits of group psychotherapy and exhibited denial of their problems. After approximately 10 sessions, however, patients became more identified with the group and started to discuss problems about the chronicity of the disorder and social adjustment. Less time was spent discussing medications and more time on interpersonal learning, instilling hope, and imparting information. Results showed marked improvements in medication adherence as measured by lithium levels and the course of disorder. In the two-year period prior to participation in the group, the sample spent an average of 16.2 weeks a year in hospital and had mean lithium levels of 0.53 mEq/l, whilst during the two years that the group functioned the sample averaged 3.2 weeks of hospitalization a year and had mean lithium levels of 0.94 mEq/l.

SECONDARY OUTCOME STUDIES

Early Studies

A study by Van Gent and Zwart (1991), which provided five theme-orientated groups for the partners of patients with bipolar disorder ($n=14$) and compared this with the usual input for partners ($n=12$), failed to show any improvement in adherence in the patients as assessed by serum lithium levels. Partners offered the active intervention attended five structured group sessions where information concerning bipolar disorder, medication, practical advice, and aspects of daily functioning were explored. Non-adherence rates did not differ for the 12 months before and after the study: in the intervention group 4/14 were non-adherent before and 3/14 after the intervention, whilst in the control group 2/12 individuals were non-adherent before and after the study period.

Clarkin *et al.* (1998) described a randomized trial of a marital intervention with the spouses of patients with bipolar disorder. Forty-two patients were randomly assigned to receive medication plus 25 sessions of a manualized psychoeducational marital therapy or medication only. Although patients in both groups received help with medication management, adherence levels (measured on a 1–6 scale) at a 11-month follow-up were significantly higher in the intervention as compared to the control group (5.7 vs 5.2, $p=0.008$).

Recent Studies

Reviews of the current developments in psychological therapies in bipolar disorders (e.g. Colom *et al.* 1998; Scott 1995; Scott and Colom 2005) suggest that most represent adaptations of the evidence-based approaches used in unipolar disorders and in schizophrenia (particularly the family therapy models). Interestingly, all these brief therapies appear to include four key components: (i) psychoeducation about the disorder; (ii) inducing lifestyle regularity (including reduction in substance use); (iii) enhancing medication adherence; and (iv) early recognition and management of symptoms of relapse. The key therapy models—namely interpersonal social rhythms therapy (IPSRT; Frank *et al.* 2000); cognitive behaviour therapy (CBT; Lam *et al.* 2003); family focused therapy (FFT; Miklowitz *et al.* 2003) or group psychoeducation (Colom *et al.* 2003a)—that have been or are currently the subject of large-scale randomized controlled trails, will briefly be discussed with particular attention to any data available on medication adherence.

Interpersonal social rhythms therapy was one of the first systematic psychological therapies developed specifically for individuals with BP. A randomized treatment trial with a two-year follow-up has reported on the first 82 participants allocated to IPSRT or intensive clinical management. The trial has two phases: an acute treatment phase and a maintenance phase, and 50% of participants in each group remain in the same treatment arm throughout the study while the remaining participants cross-over to the other treatment arm (Frank *et al.* 2000). The key findings so far are that IPSRT does induce more stable social rhythms (Frank *et al.* 1997). There were no statistically significant between-treatment differences in time to remission, but those entering the trial in a major depressive episode showed a significantly shorter time to recovery with IPSRT compared to intensive clinical management

(21 weeks vs 40 weeks; Hlastala *et al.* 1997). However, there were no between-group differences in treatment adherence levels.

Lam *et al.* (2003) reported a randomized controlled trial where 103 individuals with euthymic bipolar disorder were allocated to routine care, or routine care with a flexible schedule of 12–18 individual sessions of CBT within the first six months and 2 booster sessions in the second six months. After controlling for gender and illness history, the intervention group had significantly fewer relapses (CBT group=43%; control group=75%), psychiatric admissions (15% vs 33%) or total days in episode (about 27 days vs 88 days) over 12 months than the control group. At six months serum levels of mood stabilizer were available for 50% patients. The CBT group had significantly greater adherence on self-report measures at six-month follow-up (88% vs 67%; $p=0.02$), but the difference in serum levels (adequate levels were 93% in CBT vs 78% in control group) failed to reach statistical significance ($p=0.06$).

Miklowitz and colleagues (2000; 2003) undertook the largest trial of family focused therapy (FFT). One hundred and one participants with bipolar disorder who were receiving usual treatment were randomly allocated to 20 sessions of FFT ($n=31$) or to case management ($n=70$), which comprised 2 sessions of family psychoeducation and crisis intervention as required. Over a 12-month period, individuals receiving FFT plus usual treatment as compared to case management plus usual treatment, survived significantly longer in the community without relapsing (71% vs 47%) and showed significantly greater reductions in symptom levels. However, further analysis demonstrated that these benefits were limited to depression and there was no specific reduction in manic relapses or symptoms. Overall, the benefits of FFT were most striking in individuals living in a high expressed emotion environment. Patients assigned to the longer psychosocial treatment also had significantly lower non-adherence rates than patients assigned to the shorter intervention. Rates of partial and non-adherence were 39% and 16% in the FFT group but 34% and 45% in the control group.

The randomized controlled trial of psychoeducation in bipolar disorder by Colom *et al.* (2003a), allocated 120 euthymic bipolar subjects receiving standard treatments to either 22 sessions of a structured group psychoeducation programme, or to the equivalent number of sessions of an unstructured support group attended by the same therapists who delivered the psychotherapy intervention. The psychoeducation approach employed here was broader than that described in the studies in schizophrenia and included behavioural interventions. At two-year follow-up, the psychoeducation intervention compared with the control treatment was associated with a significant reduction in total number of relapses and 36% of patients in the control group were hospitalized compared with 8% in the psychoeducation group. Although patients in the active intervention group had significantly higher serum lithium levels than those in the control group ($p = 0.03$), Colom *et al.* (2003b) have undertaken additional studies to demonstrate that the benefits of psychoeducation are not mediated solely through enhanced adherence. In those with low levels of adherence to lithium, psychoeducation as compared to the non-specific support group intervention appears to be of benefit because it reduces the variance in lithium levels (Scott and Colom 2005).

SUMMARY OF FINDINGS IN BIPOLAR DISORDERS

The most obvious comment to make about studies in bipolar disorders is that there is a lack of rigorous or large-scale primary outcome studies. There are only two randomized controlled trials available. The one of psychoeducation, although including 60 subjects, failed to overcome the problems identified in the literature on schizophrenia regarding the need to use behavioural as well as educational interventions. As such, it is not surprising that it showed the same outcomes as noted before, namely increased knowledge without any clinically meaningful change in adherence. The other randomized controlled

Box 12 Interventions used in effective approaches to adherence in schizophrenia and bipolar disorder

Exploration of patients model of disorder with attention to cultural beliefs and context

Education regarding disorder and its treatment, provided in verbal, written, didactic, video, interactive formats

Attention to therapeutic alliance, avoiding confrontation, enhancing motivation by linking adherence to personal goals

Behavioural and concrete problem-solving strategies: using reminders, cues and reinforcements, regular medication routines, self-monitoring

Identification of attitudes and beliefs about treatment, particularly those that reduce use of coping behaviours such as adherence

Simple cognitive interventions to modify maladaptive ideas

trial is over 20-years old and included only 28 subjects. However, this study is of interest as it incorporates behavioural strategies along with interventions targeted at attitudes and beliefs to try to overcome barriers to medication adherence. This appears to be a cost-effective approach as a six-session intervention improved adherence and was associated with reduced hospitalizations. The findings in this study and the cohort study by Scott and Tacchi (2002) concur with the findings from the secondary outcome studies of broad-based brief psychological treatments for bipolar disorders, that is, interventions that incorporate educational, behavioural and/or cognitive and affective components are likely to improve medication adherence in bipolar disorders. It is interesting to note that family interventions may be helpful in bipolar disorders, although both these approaches incorporate behavioural and problem-solving strategies, which were shown to be the essential added ingredients for those family interventions that had a beneficial effect on medication adherence in schizophrenia. Rather than try to summarize the limited data available from studies, Box 12 identifies interventions that are reported in the literature on schizophrenia and bipolar disorders that may be useful strategies for improving adherence.

13

Unipolar Depression

There has been a dramatic increase in awareness of the problem of syndromal and sub-syndromal symptoms of depression in bipolar disorders depression and the significant impact these have on day-to-day functioning. As yet there are no studies in bipolar disorders exploring strategies to enhance medication adherence with the specific goal of attaining recovery or remission from depression. However, we will briefly give an overview of interventions applied to unipolar disorders in order to examine if clinicians can utilize any of the effective techniques in their routine practice.

Simply to follow advice and education has also been found to be effective in improving adherence in antidepressant treatment in primary care (Lin *et al.* 1995). One hundred and fifty-five patients receiving a new prescription for an antidepressant were interviewed by telephone at the first and fourth month after the initial prescription. Comparisons were made between those who continued antidepressants for at least 30 and 90 days and those who stopped in this time. Results showed patients receiving more educational messages concerning medication and discussions of behavioural strategies from their doctor were more likely to be adherent with medication. It is suggested that this advice is given early and repeated at later stages throughout treatment.

Robinson *et al.* (1995) observed that depressed patients who were able to use simple cognitive behavioural strategies such as planning pleasurable activities showed significantly improved adherence with antidepressant medication in the months following treatment. Patients identified from pharmacy data as receiving new prescriptions for antidepressants were invited to enter the study. The use of cognitive behavioural (CB) techniques was suggested during the primary care by

Improving Adherence in Schizophrenia and Bipolar Disorders Mary-Jane Tacchi and Jan Scott

the physician when antidepressants were first prescribed. The cognitive behavioural techniques suggested were planning activities that: (1) were pleasurable; (2) boosted confidence; (3) helped with relaxation; (4) were with other people; (5) used problem-solving techniques; or (6) recognized negative thoughts and replaced them with positive ones. At four months, patients were assessed as to whether they had recognized and utilized the interventions (high CB score) or not (low CB score). It was found that high CB scores were associated with higher levels of adherence in the first 31 days after the prescription, and that 78% of high CB score subjects reported continued use of antidepressants compared with 60% of patients with a low CB score.

Katon *et al.* (1995) compared the effectiveness of a multifaceted intervention in 119 patients with depression in primary care with the effectiveness of usual care by the primary care physician. In the intervention condition patients alternated visits with their primary care physician and with a psychiatrist over 4–6 weeks. The psychiatrist educated the patient about the biology of depression and the mechanism of action of antidepressants. Potential side effects and stressful life events were also reviewed. The intervention also utilized discussion and a short educational videotape and booklet to provide additional information. Results showed that for patients with major depression, 88% of those receiving the active intervention received an adequate dosage of antidepressants for at least 30 days compared to 57% of control subjects; at 90 days, the proportions fell slightly to 76% and 50%, respectively. The researchers concluded that the intervention significantly improved the process of care for depression and this was associated with significantly better adherence.

Peveler and colleagues (2000) undertook a randomized controlled trial of 250 patients starting treatment with a tricyclic antidepressant. Patients were assigned to groups that received: (i) an information leaflet that described the medication, unwanted effects and what to do in the event of missing a dose; (ii) medication counselling that was given by a nurse; (iii) both approaches; or (iv) usual treatment. Counselling sessions included an assessment of daily routines and lifestyle, attitudes to treatment, and understanding of the reasons for treatment. Education was given about many issues including depressive disorders, self-help and local resources, and the need to continue treatment for up to six months. The feasibility of involving family or friends with medicine taking was explored. At 12 weeks, 83% of patients with a major depressive episode who received counselling were adherent with medication compared with 52% of those receiving a leaflet and counselling, 48% of those receiving leaflet only and 33% of those receiving no intervention. The researchers concluded that information leaflets had no effect on adherence either on their own or in combination with counselling. Although the improvement in adherence produced by counselling was not matched by a significant improvement in clinical outcome or use of service in all participants, there was evidence that symptoms and health did improve in patients with more severe symptoms receiving higher doses of medication.

SUMMARY OF FINDINGS IN UNIPOLAR DISORDERS

Obviously, it is not likely that the approaches used to improve adherence in the acute treatments of unipolar disorders in primary care can be applied without modification to bipolar disorders. However, there is clearly an overlap between the interventions used and those already reported for severe mental disorders. The additional component that is worthy of note is the more proactive approach to monitoring patients and reinforcing information or checking understanding; for example through regular telephone contacts. Finally, these studies again reinforce that information alone is not a sufficient intervention when attempting to instigate a new behaviour or modify a current behaviour (Mazzuca 1982).

14

Translating Research Findings into Clinical Practice

So far, the research evidence for predictors of medication non-adherence in severe mental disorders and findings from studies of interventions that attempt to enhance adherence have been reviewed. The studies vary considerably in their size and quality, but overall there are some consistent themes regarding reasons for non-adherence and some of the interventions appear to be promising. The challenge for clinicians is to translate the research evidence into everyday clinical practice in a meaningful, effective, and practical way. There is no 'one answer' with regard to preventing or managing non-adherence. Individual clinicians will adopt different interventions depending upon a range of circumstances including their own experience and training, patient preferences, time and resource constraints.

Our primary aim should be prevention of medication non-adherence, with recognition and management of cases of non-adherence coming a close second. In order to achieve these goals, the regular assessment of adherence status and the use of simple targeted interventions will need to be part of routine clinical practice rather than the exception. All clinicians involved with treating patients need skills in this area. For many, there is no need for formal training as it simply requires a more systematic application of the skills and knowledge that they already possess. For others, courses of 1–2 days (Boilson *et al.* 2004) or of up to 10 days (Gray 2001) can provide training in the skills required to effectively tackle non-adherence in day-to-day practice.

If we now consider the evidence-base, the research on predictors indicates that adherence in schizophrenia and bipolar disorders is

Improving Adherence in Schizophrenia and Bipolar Disorders Mary-Jane Tacchi and Jan Scott

affected by a number of common factors that are amenable to modification. It is clear that a good therapeutic alliance is essential, and that patients' attitudes, beliefs and coping styles will predict their behaviour (including whether they seek help for a mental disorder and whether they adhere to treatment). That a patient's environment will affect their behaviour, particularly their living situation and relationships with significant others, and that comorbid substance misuse is commonly associated with non-adherence.

The research on interventions clearly indicates that education is not enough when given alone and, perhaps surprisingly, that family interventions (unless incorporating behavioural strategies) have not shown much benefit. The most successful interventions have consisted of a combination of styles of intervention addressing education, behaviour, and cognitions. We will now look at how to use this information to construct a systematic approach to the detection and management of non-adherence in schizophrenia and bipolar disorders.

A PATHWAY TO ADDRESS ADHERENCE

We will now outline the steps involved in addressing medication adherence. Some of these will be useful in any therapeutic encounter but some are specifically targeted at enhancing adherence. Some of the research evidence demonstrates that this issue can be tackled through the use of complex psychotherapeutic interventions provided by highly trained individuals. However, we will focus on a pathway that could be utilized by any mental health professional without further specialist training and, in doing so, make it more likely that this will be incorporated into everyday practice. The therapeutic alliance is discussed initially as this can be regarded as the key to successful interactions between the clinician and the patient. Next, we explore beliefs: first those of the clinician and then the patient's beliefs about the disorder and its treatment using the cognitive representation of illness model. The patient's previous coping strategies are examined and the effectiveness of these is considered. It is suggested that the clinician can use all this information to engage and work with the patient to incorporate both parties' goals into the treatment plan and build on the patient's model to provide a coherent strategy for any interventions, rather than providing a competing or contradictory approach. Finally, specific interventions are described that can be used to target certain behaviours or beliefs to enhance medication adherence. It is not our aim to describe more specialized techniques or approaches in detail as these are described in the treatment manuals designed for those therapies (e.g. Kemp *et al.* 1997).

However, we do include information on simple interventions that can be applied without recourse to specialist training.

The Therapeutic Alliance

A number of models have been proposed to conceptualize the therapeutic alliance. We would advise using a model with which you are already familiar, particularly if that makes sense to you and you are comfortable using it. However, if you are not used to thinking in terms of a model to help characterize your interaction with a patient, this section will highlight some of the key elements you need to take into account when establishing a healthy collaboration with a patient who you may work with over many years. We outline some of the models described in the literature, but then focus on the cognitive representation of illness model to demonstrate how this can be used to establish a positive therapeutic alliance. If you decide to adopt a new model it is important to bear in mind that it will take time to feel comfortable using this.

General Issues in Establishing an Alliance

Aspects of the doctor–patient interaction that have been described as important are affective quality and communication style (see Box 13). The affective quality of this relationship identified as particularly important includes qualities such as warmth, positive regard, lack of tension, and non-verbal expressiveness (DiMatteo 1979, Friedman 1979). Communication is an important part of the doctor–patient encounter and various styles can have a detrimental effect on the relationship; for example, an approach that assumes that the patient will unquestionably follow any advice that is given and communication that is one sided such that the patient does not feel listened to by the clinician. Svarstad

Box 13 Developing a positive therapeutic alliance

- Affective qualities: warmth, positive regard, lack of tension, non-verbal expressiveness
- Communication style: ask, not tell, listen
- Patient participation: answer patient concerns, allow discussion
- Collaboration: mutual understanding and goal setting
- Psychotherapeutic qualities: empathy and respect
- Time: do not rush

(1974) identified a number of strategies that are frequently used to control or limit patient-initiated communications, such as looking at the clock, interrupting the patient, or ignoring the patient's communication. Such tactics clearly need to be avoided, particularly as Rost (1989) found that patient's adherence was significantly related to the opportunity to answer questions that they had been asked and to offer information voluntarily.

It is important to remember the principles of ensuring mutual respect and showing empathy with the patient when trying to develop a positive therapeutic alliance. A common barrier for clinicians is a perceived shortage of time. There is no simple solution to this, but it is essential that time is spent especially with new patients to start building a rapport. The only solace we can offer busy clinicians is that the time spent establishing a collaborative relationship where both clinician and patient understand each other's views and goals is never wasted, and indeed may save several hours of work at a later time (when a disenchanted patient who has disengaged has to be re-referred to the service and/or admitted to hospital to stabilize their mental state). An important aspect of the alliance is to create an atmosphere of open, honest communication so a patient can reveal any difficulties. It is particularly important with a patient at risk of non-adherence, as any sense that their behaviour will be disapproved of is likely to lead to reluctance on the part of the patient to tell the clinician or to voice his or her concerns about treatment. The critical skill for the clinician is to focus more on asking questions and listening, and gradually 'shaping' and guiding the patient's discovery rather than telling the patient his or her views, as simply providing information does not necessarily change their view.

Models for Developing the Therapeutic Alliance

Charles *et al.* (1977) defined shared decision-making as a mechanism for decreasing the information and power asymmetry between doctors and patients by increasing patients' information, sense of autonomy and/or control over treatment decisions that effect their well-being. Hamann *et al.* (2003) discuss the use of a 'shared decision-making' to increase medication adherence. The basic elements of this approach are: that there are at least two partners involved in the decision-making process, for example patient and doctor (but also possibly nurses, family members, etc.); that all partners take steps in sharing the treatment decision; that the partners share the information about treatment options in order to arrive at a consensus regarding the preferred treatment option; and that all parties are aware of and agree the approach.

Dearing (2004) describes a model to quantify aspects of the nurse–patient relationship. She describes the core category as the concept of 'knowing' which is subcategorized into 'socializing', 'normalizing' and 'celebrating'. These categories describe interactions between nurse and patient to produce a positive therapeutic alliance and subsequently a positive influence upon treatment adherence. Alternatively, Tarrier and Barrowclough (2003) suggest the use of an 'interaction model'. They suggest that a patient acquires an individual illness model and that interventions by the clinician should take into account the patient's model and the interaction between this and the professional's beliefs in order to establish a joint view of the issues and problems.

Establishing the Therapeutic Alliance in Routine Practice

Awareness of your own beliefs and attitudes: Before eliciting the patient's beliefs it may help to reflect upon your own attitudes and behaviour. Asking someone to take medication requires him or her to adopt a new behaviour. Yet most doctors expect patients to do this without question and consider non-adherence as the abnormal behaviour. Therefore, it is useful to 'normalize' non-adherence by thinking of a new behaviour that you have tried to adopt, for example flossing your teeth or starting a new exercise regime. Then ask yourself, Why did you decide to do it? Did you stick with this new behaviour every day? How successful were you in maintaining the new behaviour? What was difficult about it? What increased your chances of success?

When we accept how difficult it is to change a specific behaviour or adopt a new behaviour for ourselves, it often helps us realize the enormous undertaking of patients who are often recommended to take medication for years or even for life. This puts into perspective the challenge we often set for our patients. The beginnings of any good therapeutic relationship start with an understanding of the problem of taking medication in reality (rather than a theoretical knowledge of the potential benefits) and an ability to empathize with the patient's predicament.

Establish the Patient's Model: As described in Part One of this book (Chapter 9), the cognitive representation of illness model can be used to conceptualize the patient's beliefs, attitudes, and coping styles. We now need to consider how to establish the patient's model of their disorder during a clinical assessment. The most direct method is to establish the patient's ideas and views about the five key areas of the model, namely:

1. Exploring identify—What is it?
2. Exploring cause—What caused it?

3. Exploring time line—How long will it last?
4. Exploring consequences—How will it affect/has it affected me?
5. Exploring cure—Can it be controlled?

The patient's views of their experiences can then be established (examples of more detailed questions are given in Box 14) and it is possible to review any gaps in their knowledge or any misunderstandings they have about the nature or cause of their difficulties. Exploring the patient's views of whether the problem can be cured or controlled also allows the clinician to establish the individual's coping style: did they show evidence of avoidance (ignoring their symptoms in the hope they would go away); did they try to actively problem solve; did they use maladaptive strategies, for example using drugs or alcohol, to try to reduce symptoms. Certain behaviours that may have seemed eccentric can be viewed as having some logic when understood from the patient's perspective. In addition, as will be discussed next, effective strategies can be encouraged and built upon by increasing the patient's perception that they have some control on their problems, and also increasing collaboration

The second component of the model allows the patient and clinician to explore coping strategies that the patient has used to date; these will relate specifically to any symptoms that have been experienced, and also their general approach to difficulties in their life. These strategies can be seen in the context of the patient's beliefs about themselves and

Box 14 Questions to establish the patient's views of their problems

- *What is it?* What brought you here today? Can you describe what is happening to you? What concerns do you have?
- *What caused it?* What do you think is happening to you? What do you think has led to this? What explanation have you considered? Has anyone else offered an explanation to you?
- *Timeline?* How long do you think this will last? What can you or anyone else do to affect this? Was there something that happened before that you can recognize?
- *How has it affected me?* What have been the consequences so far? What have been the costs to you and to others? In future how could we avoid the negative consequences?
- *Can it be controlled?* What have you done to try to control this problem? What can you or anyone else do to affect it/control it? Are there any problem-solving techniques or coping strategies that you have tried?

about the disorder. Once explored, the patient and clinician should appraise, together, how effective these have been with regard to effect upon the symptoms and the disorder. If strategies have been effective these can be incorporated into the treatment plan, for example advocating regular sleep–wake cycles to reduce instability in daily routines (that in bipolar disorders can increase the risk of relapse). If the patient's strategies have been ineffective, this information can be used to help the patient reappraise whether this is an approach that should be revised (for example the benefit of trying to 'self-medicate' mood changes with drugs or alcohol), or should be replaced with an alternative coping strategy. A patient may have tried a number of strategies, indeed the decision to seek help may be a problem-solving strategy that they only try after they have made other unsuccessful attempts to cope with their symptoms. Box 15 outlines some simple questions to help explore these issues.

Integrating the Patient's and Clinician's Goals: As has been stated, when there is coherence between the patient's concrete experience of symptoms, the meaning that they have attached to these and the explanation given to them by others, including the clinician, there is much greater likelihood of engagement and adherence with treatment. The task for the clinician is to use the patient's model as a starting point for reinforcing accurate information and perceptions, and adaptive coping strategies, using questions to guide discovery of other important facts and providing information as necessary (e.g. about whether the disorder is recurrent). In this way, the clinician uses the patient's initial model as the starting point for their discussion but then builds on this to develop an accurate shared model of the disorder. Having incorporated both the patient's and clinician's model into the formulation of the patient's problems, it is then possible to put forward a logical set of treatment goals that make sense to the patient. This should increase the

Box 15 Exploring coping strategies

- What was the first thing you did to try to cope with this problem?
- What happened as a result?
- How effective did you think that approach was?
- What (symptoms) changed as a result?
- Did you try anything else?
- How effective was that approach?
- What would you do differently next time?

acceptability of the regime to the patient and, therefore, makes it more likely it will be followed.

Some beliefs that are important to identify in patients who may need long-term treatment are their perceived susceptibility to further episodes of disorder, and their understanding or predictions of the likely severity of the consequences if this did occur (Becker and Maimon 1975). It is proposed that the individual is more likely to adhere to medication if their perception of this threat is high (threat = susceptibility plus severity) and the perceived benefits of treatment exceed the perceived barriers to engaging with treatment (Scott and Wright 1997). Beliefs associated with adherence may be specific to the illness or the treatment (e.g. doctors do more harm than good), but many represent the general rules or assumptions that operate across the whole spectrum of the individuals' life (e.g. I must be in control). Beliefs are influenced by other factors, for example personality attitudes, views of significant others, cultural beliefs, and general orientation towards medicine (Horne and Weinman 1995). Weinstein (1988) stated that an individual needs a prompt (a reminder of the threat of illness or the action that must be taken against it) to engage in health-related behaviours. These 'cues' to action can be internal such as the recognition of prodromal symptoms or external such as statements made by others. As such, it is helpful to establish the benefits and barriers to adherence with the patient (see Box 16). The skill of the clinician is to ensure that any

Box 16 Exploring benefits and barriers for adherence

Benefits of adherence

- Being symptom-free
- Enjoying hobbies, socializing, studies
- Return to usual daily activities, being able to work
- Increased concentration
- No hassle from others about taking treatment

Barriers to adherence

- Forgetting tablets/regime not fitting in with lifestyle
- Beliefs, for example I should be able to cope without tablets
- Views of significant others, for example my father took lithium and didn't like it
- Stigma of illness, for example taking tablets reminds me I have a chronic illness
- Concerns about side effects

of their interventions help the patient develop a balanced view of their prognosis and also have a positive effect on behaviour, rather than leading the patient to give up hope or engage in 'defensive avoidance' (Zygmunt *et al.* 2002). In general, this is best achieved by reinforcing positive benefits of taking medication (e.g. effective problem-solving behaviours undertaken by the patient, likelihood that adherence will increase their chances of achieving their personal goals), rather than emphasizing the negative outcomes of not taking medications (e.g. non-adherence may lead to negative family interactions).

Understanding the patient's beliefs in these areas, a realistic appraisal of the effects of the illness, exploring the presence of modifying factors, and identifying what cues a patient responds to, will allow understanding of non adherence. This, in turn, will establish what specific interventions will effect change in adherence behaviour, for example education about illness, behavioural modification or challenging cognitions.

Reducing the Risks of Non-Adherence

Monitor Adherence and Check Pattern of Adherence

The most important approach to minimizing the risk of non-adherence is for clinicians to recognize that it is likely to be a problem for all patients receiving long-term treatment at some point. Bearing this in mind, it is possible to identify some simple interventions that can be used to try to ensure adherence with newly prescribed treatments. In the first instance it is helpful to:

- Emphasize that medication is only one part of the treatment programme
- Link adherence with medication to the patient's personal goals, for example, 'if we can stabilize your mood state with medication this will give us a window of opportunity to work on how you handle your relationship with XXX, that you tell me is causing you concern…'
- Reinforce that you are keen to develop a regime that is acceptable, understandable, and manageable for the individual
- Use the minimum possible number of medications and doses
- Regularly review benefits of and barriers to adherence
- Expect non-adherence

It is useful to remember that adherence is unlikely to be an all or nothing phenomenon. Some patients take their medication regularly, others miss some doses, and others show cycles of adherence where they take treatment regularly when they feel unwell but become less strict when they feel better. It is important to repeat the question about adherence on a regular basis, but as noted before, the clinician should try to do so in a non-judgemental way so that the patient feels able to give accurate answers to the questions posed. Box 17 offers suggestions of different questions that can be used depending on the patient and the different situations in which the interviews will take place.

If there appears to be evidence of non-adherence or the patient is perceived to be at high risk of becoming non-adherent, it is helpful to establish the actual pattern of adherence, in order to intervene effectively and appropriately. The problems inherent in relying on self-report have been mentioned. However, in the context of a collaborative alliance between patient and clinician this should be less of a problem. Diary keeping or enlisting significant others to provide information may be helpful in some cases. It is good clinical practice to establish patterns of adherence right at the beginning of prescribing any medication and to encourage patients to continue to monitor this throughout treatment; for example by the use of a calendar. This will prevent an accusatory feel from discussions at a later date, as both the clinician and the patient can examine the evidence from a diary if non-adherence is a risk.

It is worth considering the nature or possible drivers of medication non-adherence when trying to determine the techniques to overcome this problem. Scott (1999) distinguishes between non-intentional and intentional non-adherence, which require different approaches. Non-intentional non-adherence usually occurs when patients forget medications or find it difficult to establish regular patterns of adherence. A review of records of taking medication may, however, expose a different type of problem, namely that certain situations increase the individual's risk for non-adherence or that the primary problem relates to attitudes rather than establishing a pattern of behaviour.

Box 17 Questions to establish or monitor adherence

- Many individuals find it hard to stick to a course of tablets—Do you ever have any trouble taking all of your medication as prescribed?
- Are there times when it is more difficult to remember to take your medication?
- Does your medication regime fit in with your lifestyle or activities?
- Do you ever try to cope without your tablets?

Intentional non-adherence is usually an indication of cognitive barriers to engaging with medication, such as beliefs that trying harder would allow the individual to deal with the symptoms without recourse to the health services.

Specific Interventions

Education: We have shown education alone is a necessary part of treatment, but on its own is not sufficient to establish adherence behaviour. The principles when providing education or imparting knowledge to the patient again is to ask, not tell. It is useful to start with the patient's own knowledge, exploring symptoms, effects on lifestyle, experience of treatment and outcome, and understanding and consequences of illness (see Box 18). For example, in offering a prescription for a particular medication it is useful to establish if the patient has heard of the medication, do they know anyone else who has taken it or a similar medication, what do they know about it, do they have any concerns about it, etc. This approach, followed by fielding any specific questions and filling in gaps in knowledge or correcting misconceptions, is usually far more effective in engaging the patient with the treatment, than the clinician giving a brief didactic presentation on the medication in question accompanied by a prescription (5% of which are never taken to the pharmacy for dispensing).

Questions are encouraged and specific information can be given with regard to illness type and treatments at regular intervals. Educational strategies need to include checks on the patient's understanding of what has been imparted, with repetitions of the information during interviews, provision of education both orally and in written formats, and regular follow-up reviews of what has been learnt. Encouraging

Box 18 Important aspects of providing education

- First find out what the patient knows
- Use simple everyday language
- Limit instructions or information to three or four major points per discussion
- Repeat and reinforce information, by recapping and giving regular summaries
- Use written materials as a supplement to oral instructions
- Check that the patient understands any information given, by asking them questions

patients to write down questions to bring along to appointments is also worthwhile. Again, whilst this may seem time-consuming, the evidence suggests this is of benefit to engaging the patient in treatment. It is important that education is understandable to the patient and is provided in terms that are appropriate to the individual—in general it is better to use simple everyday language (Atreja *et al.* 2005). Unsurprisingly, research has shown that patients who do not understand the instructions about medication are less likely to adhere to it (Svarstad 1974).

Any medication regime must be acceptable, understandable, and manageable for that particular individual. If any of these three criteria are not met, the clinician needs to ask themselves why they are letting the patient leave the consultation as there is less than a 30% likelihood that the patient will adhere with that medication (Scott 2000).

Behavioural Interventions: Unintentional non-adherence is likely to respond to a behavioural approach but in practice all forms of non-adherence will initially be tackled with behavioural approaches (Box 19).

Highly complex treatment regimens can increase the risk of non-adherence so a simple schedule should be negotiated wherever possible (Goodwin and Jamison 1990). Use of once-a-day medication or longer-acting medications should be considered if preferred by the patient. Use of a medi-pack or dosette that allows the daily medication regime to be organized in advance and self-monitoring of adherence is also helpful. Matching the prescription to the patient's lifestyle or activities and concordance with the patient's preferences with regard

Box 19 Behavioural techniques

- Give written instructions
- Use prompts, for example notes stuck in prominent places, text message alerts
- Pair tablet-taking with routine activities, for example brushing teeth
- Rehearse each step of adherence with the regime, particularly when anticipating exposure to high-risk situations where non-adherence is likely
- Engage families, significant others or support workers in the process
- Keep a diary
- Simplify the regime
- Match the prescription to the patient's lifestyle

to dosing regimes should also be considered. Lastly, discussing patient preferences for the type of drug or mode of administration (oral, depot) usually increases the likelihood of adherence.

The use of long-acting injectable medication in some circumstances can improve adherence by dispensing with the need to remember daily tablet-taking regimes. Keith and Kane (2003) suggest that patients showing partial adherence with antipsychotic medication should be considered for and/or offered treatment with a long-acting injectable atypical antipsychotic. However, we would emphasize that the ideal is to give the patient the information about the advantages and disadvantages of this treatment and offer the option of a trial of this approach. It is interesting that many patients do actively choose this approach, although others feel it takes away their autonomy. It is recognized that although depot antipsychotics cannot eliminate non-adherence they do prevent covert non-adherence (Valenstein *et al.* 2001). It seems that whilst there are advantages for some people in this method of administration, it is likely that interventions to target adherence will be required as well.

Use of medication can be improved by writing the essential details on a small card that can be carried in a pocket or wallet. This may include information about the regime, situations or symptoms that may prompt changes in medication dose and recommended action if a dose or doses of medication are missed, plus what action to take or who to contact in a crisis.

Other behavioural interventions include prompts or cues to action and the use of reinforcements or pairing medication routines with other regular activities (Scott and Wright 1997). For example, notes stuck in a prominent place that is visited daily such as the bathroom mirror may act as a reminder to take morning doses of medication. Pairing tablet-taking with a routine daily activity, for example brushing teeth, may also aid adherence. Reminders provided in real time such as prearranged telephone calls, text messaging, or using the alarm clock functions on mobile phones or other electronic equipment can help. Rehearsal, where the patient visualizes each step in their medication routine and rehearsing additional coping strategies for novel situations, is also beneficial. Family members or significant others can be engaged to offer reinforcement; however, this should only be considered when relationships are stable and the patient feels this would be constructive rather than undermining their independence.

The benefits of each strategy can be monitored through keeping a simple medication diary that can be reviewed with the clinician to monitor progress and the effectiveness of the intervention. For some of these interventions it may be possible to recruit the help of the clinical pharmacist or another team member to reinforce these strategies when prescriptions are collected.

Cognitive Techniques: Cognitive techniques will be useful particularly when non-adherence is intentional (Box 20). With intentional non-adherence the patient should be provided with a realistic appraisal of the disorder and his or her prognosis. This can take the form of an educational discussion supplemented by reading or video material. A worthwhile approach is to ask the patient to take the first step and seek information about the disorder as a homework assignment by obtaining leaflets from appropriate organizations, audiovisual aids, or the Internet, etc. Obviously this strategy can only be implemented if the clinician judges this approach would be a positive experience and within the capability of a particular individual.

The next task is to explore the individual pattern of non-adherence. This information is mainly used to identify specific situations where there is a high risk of omitting prescribed medication. When negative thoughts are noted with regard to medication these can be explored within the consultation. Again the emphasis is on guiding the patient to examine his or her own cognitions. Alternative explanations and rating of the degree of belief and thoughts needs to be generated by the patient and not the doctor. Experiments are devised to test out the negative thoughts and can also provide further data on which to base discussions to generate alternative views.

The approach taken will vary with the point in the patient's history at which non-adherence occurs. The patient who has relapsed as a result of stopping medication may be the easiest to engage in a discussion about the costs and benefits of treatment, as difficulties are fresh and tangible.

Box 20 Cognitive techniques

- Explore understanding
- Realistic appraisal of progress—education or as a homework assignment by the patient
- Explore pattern of non-adherence
- Identify negative thoughts associated with medication taking or disorder
- Test out the outcomes of negative thoughts as an experiment
- Facilitate the patient in identifying alternative explanations to modify these thoughts
- Help the patient reframe general views, for example attitudes and expectations of treatment

However, the reasons for stopping medication need to be explored as these may establish possible barriers to treatment in the future.

For patients experiencing their first psychotic episode it is likely that this is also the first occasion they have contact with mental health services. There is no past pattern with regard to medication adherence to review and some of the discussion will be hypothetical, trying to establish general attitudes towards medication and likely behaviours, and potential periods of increased risk of non-adherence. In trying to encourage adherence, it is important to strike a balance between instilling hope about future prospects for remission and/or a good quality of life despite being diagnosed as having a severe mental disorder, against warnings about the adverse effects of non-adherence on prognosis, which may demoralise the individual because it emphasizes the negative impact of the disorder on the individual's adult life.

A different scenario is a patient on maintenance treatment who is currently well. It is common in this instance for a patient to start to doubt the benefits of or necessity of treatment. In this case, a constructive way forward is to discuss the costs and benefits of medication and to undertake a careful assessment of knowledge about the difference between the treatment of acute symptoms, as compared with treatments that prevent symptom return or keep people well. This may also require a review of the initial presentation and rationale for treatment. This can sometimes be difficult as memories of a past relapse have faded or are being avoided. Reality testing perhaps by involving significant others or gaining information from other sources, for example the Internet, may be useful.

Consideration should be given to the patient who refuses medication, but is prepared to remain in contact with the clinic. There are many reasons why a patient decides not to engage in treatment, some of which include a poor doctor–patient relationship, a decision made whilst being unwell, side effects of medication, media reports of negative effects such as suggestions of dependency, the views of significant others, or a reduction in insight. If it is possible to identify a specific reason, this can be amenable to intervention using the behavioural and cognitive strategies identified. However, in some instances, particularly if the patient has the mental capacity to make this decision, it may be necessary as a clinician to agree with the patient to a period of non treatment as an experiment. Whilst unlikely to be the clinician's preferred course of action, it is better to help manage this process rather than seeing the patient vote with their feet and leave the service entirely, and risk sudden medication withdrawal and early symptomatic relapse. Maintaining regular, indeed ideally, increased contact with the patient has the advantage of keeping the dialogue open with the prospect of a return to medication without this decision being seen as a failure on anyone's part.

The patient who is refusing treatment should also be encouraged to review his or her decision by listing advantages and disadvantages of the choice, and considering if there is anything else that might change his or her mind and lead to continued acceptance of medication. Patients should be encouraged to talk to others to check out their views and to read about what interventions might protect them from relapse. If a patient is to stop medication, it is crucial they are given advice to do this slowly and to avoid using non-prescription drugs in their place.

If the patient chooses to stop medication then it is important that both parties plan the medication withdrawal programme, the length of time this medication-free experiment will last, the frequency of reviews, and the success criteria for this experiment. Importantly, both parties must also agree in advance how to identify the end point of an unsuccessful experiment, i.e. under what circumstances would the patient accept medication again. Patients should be encouraged to regularize their day-to-day activities and utilize any other strategies that may control symptoms. A record should then be kept of symptoms and agreed outcomes to make an accurate assessment of progress, and the patient is also encouraged to be honest in consultations with regard to their well-being and behaviour. Ideally, the patient should also identify someone outside the services they trust who will also help monitor their progress and can advocate on their behalf, particularly if they experience symptoms of a recurrence. At this point, the clinician will hopefully have a further opportunity to negotiate a further treatment trial using a regime that the patient believes is acceptable, understandable, and manageable.

15

Final Comments

This book has explored the key evidence for predictors of non-adherence in severe mental disorders and the interventions that may increase adherence. We have also tried to identify which interventions employed in research settings can be employed in day-to-day clinical practice. It is, however, important to acknowledge that the research in this area is in its infancy. Psychiatry has been slow to recognize the problem of non-adherence, and even slower to understand that tackling this problem is more complex than simply prescribing an effective dose of a medication that reportedly has a benign side-effect profile. Sadly, the non-adherence rate is still likely to be 30–50% and if the treatment is offered over a long term, the patient is likely to stop the medication against medical advice on one or two occasions over 12–24 months. As such, clinicians cannot ignore this issue: there is no such treatment as medication alone.

Clinicians need to invest time in establishing a therapeutic alliance with their patients who have schizophrenia and bipolar disorders. They need to develop a shared understanding of the problems presented and what interventions would be acceptable before they can move to the point of prescribing an evidence-based treatment. Clinicians might argue that some patients will not take medication despite a positive therapeutic relationship; however, it is perhaps more pertinent to note that very few patients who report a negative alliance will adhere to effective treatments. If a positive working relationship is established, the acceptability and manageability of the medication regime for the individual patient will dictate which treatment option is selected. Trying to establish positive reasons to accept the treatment, such as linking medication adherence to personal goals (such as a return to work), is more likely to

Improving Adherence in Schizophrenia and Bipolar Disorders Mary-Jane Tacchi and Jan Scott

be effective than negative statements about the likelihood of involuntary hospitalization if the patient is non-adherent. The latter approach is often regarded by patients as punitive and may adversely affect the therapeutic alliance. Being vigilant for signs of ambivalence about treatment, and repeatedly checking out that patients understand the nature of the disorder and the rationale for medication, will hopefully avert a number of instances of non-adherence. However, as this problem is highly likely to occur, it is useful to spend some time developing a hierarchy of simple interventions that can be incorporated into routine practice to try to overcome non-adherence. We have tried to demonstrate that in many instances the interventions simply represent the attitudes, skills and knowledge already possessed by clinicians, or are techniques that can be learnt and employed without major disruption to the clinicians' style and mode of practice.

Weiss *et al.* (2002) estimated that it takes about six months to establish adherence in a patient starting treatment with antipsychotic medication, and about 13 months for a patient who is currently adherent to become non-adherent. If the clinician is sensitive to the risk factors for individual non-adherence, such as attitudes or beliefs about the disorder and its treatment, and takes these into account at the start of the working relationship with a patient, it is likely they can reduce the time taken to establish the patient on a therapeutic dose of medication. The fact that it may take over a year for a patient to become non-adherent after they have been established on medication should encourage clinicians that the management approaches we have described can be utilized in their clinical practice. Provided the clinician carefully monitors interactions and interviews for warning signs that the patient is becoming non-adherent, it seems there is ample time to undertake a hierarchy of interventions to modify this behaviour. Weiden and Olfson (1995) estimated that reducing non-adherence rates by 50% would lead to a reduction in one-year hospitalization rates of 12% together with marked improvements in other clinical outcomes and social adjustment, as well as reducing the burden and stress experienced by the patients' family. In addition, it would undoubtedly reduce some of the workload of clinicians treating individuals with severe mental disorders, so there are likely to be some benefits to clinicians in taking a more systematic approach to this problem.

References

Adams J and Scott J. Predicting medication adherence in severe mental disorders. *Acta Psychiatr Scand*, 2000; **101**: 119–124.

Altamura AC and Mauri MC. Plasma Concentrations Information and therapy adherence during long-term treatment with antidepressants. *Br J Clin Pharmacol*, 1985; **20**: 714–716.

Atkinson JM, Coia DA, Gilmour WH *et al.* The impact of education groups for people with schizophrenia on social functioning and quality of life. *Br J Psychiatry*, 1996; **168**: 199–204.

Atreja A, Bellam N and Levy SR. Strategies to enhance patient adherence: Making it simple. *Gen Med*, 2005; **7** (1).

Azrin NH and Teichner G. Evaluation of an instructional program for improving medication compliance for chronically mentally ill outpatients. *Behaviour Res Ther*, 1998; **36**: 849–861.

Bauml J, Kissling W and Pitschel WG. Psychoedukative Gruppen Fur schizophrenie Patienten: Einfluss auf Wissensstand und Compliance. *Nervenheilkunde*, 1996; **15**: 145–150.

Bech P, Vendesborg P and Rafaelsen O. Lithium maintenance treatment of manic-melancholic patients: Its role in the daily routine. *Acta Psychiatr Scand*, 1976; **53**: 70–81.

Beck AT, Rush AJ, Shaw BF *et al. Cognitive Therapy of Depression*, Guilford Press, New York, 1979.

Becker MH and Maiman LA. Sociobehavioural determinants of compliance with health and medical care recommendations. *Medical Care*, 1975; **13**: 10–24.

Begley CE, Annegers JF, Swann AC *et al.* The lifetime cost of bipolar disorder in the US: An estimate for new cases in 1988. *Pharmacoeconomics*, 2001; **19**: 483–495.

Boczkowski JA, Zeichner A and DeSanto N. Neuroleptic compliance among chronic schizophrenic outpatients: An intervention outcome report. *J Consult Clin Psychol*, 1995; **5** (53): 666–671.

Bond GR, Miller LD, Krumwied RD *et al.* Assertive case management in three CMHCs: A controlled study. *Hosp Community Psychiatry*, 1988; **39**: 411–418.

Brown CS, Wright RG and Christensen DB. Association between type of medication instruction and patients' knowledge, side effects, and compliance. *Hosp Community Psychiatry*, 1987; **38**: 55–60.

Buchanan A. A two year prospective study of treatment compliance in patients with schizophrenia. *Psychol Med*, 1992; **22** (3): 787–797.

Buckley P, Cannon M and Larkin C. Abuse of neuroleptic drugs. *Br J Addict*, 1991; **86**: 789–790.

Bush CT, Langford MW, Rosen P *et al.* Operation outreach: Intensive case management for severely psychiatrically disabled adults. *Hosp Community Psychiatry*, 1990; **41**: 647–649.

Cannon M and Jones P. Neuroepidemiology: Schizophrenia. *J Neurol Neurosurg Psychiatry*, 1996; **61**: 604–613.

Carrick R, Mitchell A, Powell RA *et al.* The quest for well-being: A qualitative study of the experience of taking antipsychotic medication. *Psychol Psychother: Theory, Res Prac*, 2004; **77** (1): 19–33.

Charles C, Gafni A and Whelan T. Shared decision-making in the medical encounter: What does it mean? (or it takes at least two to tango). *Soc Sci Med*, 1977; **44**: 681–692.

Clarkin J, Carpenter D, Hull J *et al.* Effects of psycho-educational intervention for married patients with bipolar disorders and their spouses. *Psychiatr Serv*, 1998; **49**: 531–533.

Cochran S. Preventing medication non-compliance in the out-patient treatment of bipolar affective disorder. *J Consult Clin Psychol*, 1984; **52**: 873–878.

Cochran SD and Gitlin MJ. Attitudinal correlates of lithium compliance in bipolar affective disorders. *J Nerv Ment Dis*, August 1998; **176** (8): 457–464.

Cohen NL, Ross C, Bagby M *et al.* The 5-factor model of personality and antidepressant medication compliance. *Can J Psychiatry*, 2004; **49** (2): 106–113.

Coldham EL, Addington J and Addington D. Medication adherence of individuals with a first episode of psychosis. *Acta Psychiatr Scand*, 2002; **106**: 286–290.

Colom F and Vieta E. Treatment adherence in bipolar patients. *Clin Approaches Bipolar Disorders*, 2002; **1**: 49–56.

Colom F, Vieta E, Martinez A *et al.* What is the role of psychotherapy in the treatment of bipolar disorder? *Psychother Psychosom*, 1998; **67**: 3–9.

Colom F, Vieta E, Martinez-Aran A *et al.* Clinical factors associated with treatment non-compliance in euthymic bipolar patients. *J Clin Psychiatry*, 2000; **61**: 549–555.

Colom F, Vieta E, Martinez-Aran A *et al.* A randomised trial on the efficacy of group psychoeducation in the prophylaxis of recurrences in bipolar patients whose disease is in remission. *Arch Gen Psychiatry*, 2003a; **60** (4): 402–407.

Colom F, Eduard V, Reinares M *et al.* Psychoeducation efficacy in bipolar disorders: Beyond compliance enhancement. *J Clin Psychiatry*, 2003b; **64** (9): 1101–1105.

Connelly CE, Davenport YB and Nurnberger JI. Adherence to treatment regimen in a lithium carbonate clinic. *Arch Gen Psychiatry*, 1982; **39**: 585–588.

Corrigan PW, McCracken SG and Holmes EP. Motivational interviews as goal assessment for persons with psychiatric disability. *Community Ment Health J*, 2001; **37** (2): 113–122.

Cramer JA and Rosenheck R. Enhancing medication compliance for people with serious mental illness. *J Nerv Ment Dis*, 1999; **187**: 53–55.

Curson DA, Barnes TRE, Bamber RW *et al.* Long-term depot maintenance of chronic schizophrenic out-patients: The seven year follow up of the Medical Research Council Fluphenazine/Placebo Trial. *Br J Psychiatry*, 1985; **146**: 464–480.

Daltroy LH, Katz JN, Morlino CI *et al.* Improving doctor patient communication. *Psychiatr Med*, 1991; **2**: 31–35.

Danion J, Neunreuther C, Kreiger-Finance F *et al.* Compliance with long-term lithium treatment in major affective disorders. *Pharmacopsychiatry*, 1987; **20**: 230–231.

Das Gupta RD and Guest JF. Annual cost of bipolar disorder to UK society. *Br J Psychiatry*, 2002; **180**: 227–233.

Dearing KS. Getting it, together: How the nurse patient relationship influences treatment compliance for patients with schizophrenia. *Arch Psychiatr Nurs*, 2004; **18** (5): 155–163.

Diaz E, Levine HB, Sullivan MC, Sernyak MJ *et al.* Use of the medication event monitoring system to estimate medication compliance in patients with schizophrenia. *J Psychiatr Neurosci*, 2001; **26**: 352–359.

Dickson WE and Kendall RE. Does maintenance lithium therapy prevent recurrences of mania under ordinary clinical conditions? *Psychol Med*, 1986; **16**: 521–530.

DiMatteo MR. A social-psychological analysis of physician patient rapport: Toward a science of the art of medicine. *J Soc Issues*, 1979; **35**: 12–33.

Dixon L, Weiden P, Torres M *et al.* Assertive community treatment and medication compliance in the homeless mentally ill. *Am J Psychiatry*, 1997; **154**: 1302–1304.

Dolder CR, Lacro JP, Leckband S *et al.* Interventions to improve antipsychotic medication adherence: Review of recent literature. *J Clin Psychopharmacol*, August 2003; **23** (4): 389–399.

Dolder CR, Lacro JP, Warren KA *et al.* Brief evaluation of medication influences and beliefs: Development and testing of a brief scale for medication adherence. *J Clin Psychopharmacol*, 2002; **24** (4): 404–409.

Donohoe G, Owens N, O'Donnel C, *et al.* Predictors of compliance with neuroleptic medication among impatients with schizophrenia; a discriminant function analysis. *Eur. Psychiatry*, 2002; **16**: 293–298.

Durrenberger S, Rogers T, Walker R *et al.* Economic grand rounds: High costs of care for four patients with mania who were not compliant with treatment. *Psychiatr Serv*, December 1999; **50** (12): 1539–1542.

Eckman TA, Liberman RP, Phipps CC *et al.* Teaching medication management skills to schizophrenic patients. *J Clin Psychopharmacol*, 1990; **10**: 33–38.

Ekselius L, Bengtsson F, von Knorring L. Non-compliance with pharmacotherapy of depression is associated with a sensation seeking personality. *Int Clin Psychopharmacol*, 2000; **15** (5): 273–278.

Falloon MD, Jeffrey L, Boyd L *et al.* Family management in the prevention of morbidity of schizophrenia. *Arch Gen Psychiatry*, 1985; **42** (9): 881–896.

Falvo DR. Effective Patient Education. A Guide to Increased Compliance. Gaithersburg, Maryland. Aspen Publication Inc, 1994.

Fenton W. Shared decision making. A model for the physician-patient relationship in the 21st century? *Acta Psychiatr Scand*, 2003; **107**: 401–402.

Fenton WS, Biller CR and Heinssen RK. Determinants of medication compliance in schizophrenia: Empirical and clinical findings. *Schizophrenia Bull*, 1997; **23**: 637–651.

Ferrier NI, Stanton B, Kelly T and Scott J. Neuropsychological function in euthymic bipolar patients. *Br J Psychiatry* 1999; **175**: 246–251.

Fleischhacker W, Cozobor P, Hummer M *et al*. Placebo or active control trials of antipsychotic drugs? *Arch Gen Psychiatry*, 2003; **60** (5): 458–464.

Fleishman M. Issues in psychopharmacosocioeconomics. *Psychiatr Serv*, 2002; **53**: 1532–1534.

Ford R, Beadsmore A, Ryan P *et al*. Providing the safety net: Case management for people with serious mental illness. *J Ment Health*, 1995; **1**: 91–97.

Frank E, Hlastala S, Ritenour A *et al*. Inducing lifestyle regularity in recovering bipolar disorder patients: Results from the maintenance therapies in bipolar disorder protocol. *Biol Psychiatry*, 1997; **41** (12): 1165–1173.

Frank E, Kupfer DJ, Ehlers CK *et al*. Interpersonal and social rhythm therapy for bipolar disorder: Integrating interpersonal and behavioural approaches. *Behav Ther*, 1994; **17**: 143–149.

Frank E, Perel JM, Mallinger AG *et al*. Relationship of pharmacologic compliance to long-term prophylaxis in recurrent depression. *Psychopharmacol Bull*, 1992; **28**: 231–235.

Frank E, Swartz HA and Kupfer DJ. Interpersonal and social rhythm therapy; managing the chaos of bipolar disorder. *Biol Psychiatry*, 2000; **48** (6): 593–604.

Franks MA, Macritchie KAN and Young AH. The consequences of suddenly stopping [SS144]psychotropic medication in bipolar disorder. *Clin Approaches Bipolar Disorders*, 2005; **4**: 11–17.

Freudenreich O, Cather C, Evins AE *et al*. Attitudes of schizophrenia outpatients toward psychiatric medications: Relationship to clinical variables and insight. *J Clin Psychiatry*, October 2004; **65** (10): 1372–1376.

Friedman HS. Non-verbal communication between patients and medical practitioners. *J Soc Issues*, 1979; **35**: 82–99.

Gasquet S, Tcherny-Lessenot N, Rost JP *et al*. Patient satisfaction with antipsychotic treatment as a measure of treatment effectiveness: Results from a longitudinal study of French patients with schizophrenia. *16th Annual*. European College of Neuropsychophrmacology. 20–24 September 2003; Prague, Czech Republic.

Gengo F, Frazer A, Ramsey TA *et al*. The lithium ratio as a guide to patient compliance. *Comprehensive Psychiatry*, 1980; **21**: 276–280.

Gilbert J, Evans C, Haynes R *et al*. Predicting compliance in family practice. *Can Med Assoc J*, 1980; **123**: 119–122.

Gilmer TP, Dolder CR, Lacro JP *et al*. Adherence to treatment with antipsychotic medication and health care costs among medicaid beneficiaries with schizophrenia. *Am J Psychiatry*, April 2004; **161** (4): 692–699.

Glick ID, Clarkin JF, Haas GL *et al.* A randomised clinical trial of inpatient family intervention, VI: Mediating variables and outcome. *Fam Process*, 1991; **30**: 85–99.

Goldman CR and Quinn FL. Effects of a patient education program in the treatment of schizophrenia. *Hosp Commun Psychiatry*, 1988; **39**: 282–286.

Goodwin FK and Jamison KR. *Manic-Depressive Illness*, 1990 New York: Oxford University Press.

Goulet J, Lalonde P, Lavoe G *et al.* The impact of a neuroleptic education program on young adults with psychosis. *Can J Psychiatry*, 1993; **38**: 571–573.

Gray R. A randomised controlled trial of medication management training for CPNs. *Institute of Psychiatry. Kings College*, 2001.

Gray R, Robson D and Bressington D. Medication management for people with a diagnosis of schizophrenia. *Nurs Times*, 2002; **98** (47): 38–40.

Gray R, Wykes T and Gournay K. From compliance to concordance: A review of the literature on interventions to enhance compliance with antipsychotic medication. *J Psychiatr Ment Health Nurs*, 2002; **9**: 277–284.

Greenhouse N, Meyers B and Johnson S. Coping and medication adherence in bipolar disorders. *J Affect Disord*, 2000; **59**: 237–241.

Grunebaum MF, Weiden Peter J and Olfson M. Medication supervision and adherence of persons with psychotropic disorders in residential treatment settings: A pilot sudy. *J Clin Psychiatry*, 2001; **62**: 5.

Guimon L, Egulluz I and Bulbena A. Group pharmacotherapy in schizophrenics: Attitudinal and clinical changes. *European J Psychiatry*, 1993; **7**: 147–154.

Gupta S. Illness beliefs, compliance and treatment issues in Indian bipolar patients. *Bipolar Disord*, **7** (Suppl. 2): 27–117.

Guscott R and Taylor L. Lithium prophylaxis in recurrent affective illness efficacy, effectiveness and efficiency. *Br J Psychiatry*, 1994; **164**: 741–746.

Haas GL, Glick ID, Clarkin ID. *et al.* Inpatient family intervention: A randomised clinical trial: II Results at hospital discharge. *Arch Gen Psychiatry*, 1988; **45** (3): 217–224.

Hamann J, Leucht S and Kissling W. Shared decision making in psychiatry. *Acta Psychiatr Scand*, 2003; **107**: 403–409.

Harvey NS and Peet M. Lithium Maintenance: 2. Effects of personality and attitude on health information acquisition and compliance. *Br J Psychiatry*, 1991; **158**: 200–204.

Hattenschwiler J, Primz-Kaltenborn R, Beuenschwander M. *et al.* Illness concept and compliance with olanzapine in schizophrenic patients. ECNP 16th Annual Conference.

Haynes RB, McDonald H, Garg AX. *et al.* Interventions for helping patients to follow prescriptions for medications. Cochrane Database Syst Rev. 2002;

Haynes RB, Taylor DW and Sackett DL. *Compliance in Health Care*. Baltimore Md: John Hopkins University Press, 1979:1–18. .

Hayward P, Chan N, Kemp R *et al.* Predicting the revolving door phenomenon among patients with schizophrenia, schizoaffective, and affective disorders. *Am J Psychiatry*, 1995; **152**: 856–861.

Heinssen RK. Improving medication compliance of a patient with schizophrenia through collaborative behavioural therapy. *Psychiatr Serv*, 2002; **53** (3).

Herz MI. Psychosocial treatment. *Psychiatr Ann*, 1996; **26**: 531–535.

Hirsfeld DR, Gould RA, Reilly-Harrington NA. *et al.* Cognitive behavioural group therapy for bipolar disorder: A controlled trial. November 1998.

Hlastala SA, Frank E, Mallinger AG, *et al.* Bipolar depression: an underestimated treatment challenge. *Depression & Anxiety*, 1997; **5** (2): 73–83.

Hofer A, Kemmler G, Eder U *et al.* Attitudes toward antipsychotics among outpatient clinic attendees with schizophrenia. *J Clin Psychiatry* 2002; **63** (1): 49–53.

Hogarty GE, Andeson CM, Reiss DJ *et al.* Family psychoeducation, social skills training, and maintenance chemotherapy in the aftercare treatment of schizophrenia. *Arch Gen Psychiatry*, 1991; **48**: 340–347.

Hogarty GE, Kornblith SJ, Greenwald D *et al.* Three-year trials of personal therapy among schizophrenic patients living with or independent of family, I: Description of study and effects on relapse rates. *Am J Psychiatry*, 1997; **154**: 1504–1513.

Holzinger A, Loffler W, Muller P *et al.* Subjective Illness Theory and Antipsychotic Medication Compliance by Patients with Schizophrenia. *J Nerv Ment Dis*, 2002; **190** (9): 597–603.

Horne R and Weinman J. *The Beliefs About Medication Questionnaire: A New Measure for Assessing Lay Beliefs About Medicines*, London: Bps, 1995.

Hunt GE, Bergen J and Bashir M. Medication compliance and comorbid substance abuse in schizophrenia: Impact on community survival 4 years after relapse. *Schizophrenia Res*, 2002; **54** (3): 253–264.

Jamison KR and Akiskal HS. Medication compliance in patients with bipolar disorder. *Psychiatr Clin North Am*, 1983; **6**: 175–192.

Jamison KR, Gener RH and Goodwin FK. Patient and physician attitudes toward lithium: Relationship to compliance. *Arch Gen Psychiatry*, 1979; **36**: 866–869.

Jeste SD, Patterson TL, Palmer BW *et al.* Cognitive predictors of medication adherence among middle-aged and older outpatients with schizophrenia. *Schizophrenia Res*, 2003; **63** (1–2): 49–58.

Johnson DAW and Freedman H. Drug Defaulting by patients on long-acting phenothiazines. *Psychol Med*, 1973; **3**: 115–119.

Johnson R and McFarland B. Lithium use and discontinuation in a health maintenance organisation. *Am J Psychiatry*, 1998; **153**: 993–1000.

Judd LL, Schettler PJ, Akiskal HS *et al.* Long-term symptomatic status of bipolar I vs. bipolar II disorders. *Int J Neuropsychopharmacol*, June, 2003; **6** (2): 127–137.

Kane JM. Strategies for improving compliance in treatment of schizophrenia by using a long acting formulation of an antipsychotic: clinical studies. *J clin Psychiatry*, 2003; **64** (16): 34–40.

Kane J, Riften A, Quitkin F *et al.* Fluphenazine vs. placebo in first episode schizophrenia. *Arch Gen Psychiatry*, 1982; **39**: 70–73.

Katon W, Von Korff M, Lin E *et al.* Adequacy and duration of antidepressant treatment in primary care. *Med Care*, 1992; **30**: 67–76.

Katon W, Von Korff M, Lin E *et al*. Collaborative management to achieve treatment guidelines. *J Am Med Assoc*, 1995; **273**: 1026–1031.

Keck PE Jr, McElroy SL, Strakowski SM *et al*. Compliance with maintenance treatment in bipolar disorder. *Psychopharmacol Bull*, 1997; **33** (1): 87–91.

Keck P, Mcelroy B, Strakowski S *et al*. Factors associated with pharmacological non-compliance in patients with mania. *J Clin Psychiatry*, 1998; **57**: 292–297.

Keith SJ and Kane JM. Partial compliance and patient consequences in schizophrenia: Our patients can do better. *J Clin Psychiatry*, 2003; **64** (11): 1308–1315.

Keller M, Lavori P, Mueller T *et al*. Time to recovery, chronicity, and levels of psychopathology in major depression. A 5 year prospective follow up of 431 subjects. *Arch Gen Psychiatry*, 1992; **49**: 809–816.

Kelly GR and Scott JE. Medication compliance and health education among outpatients with chronic mental disorders. *Med Care*, 1990; **28**: 1181–1197.

Kemp R and David A. Psychological predictors of insight and compliance in psychotic patients. *Br J Psychiatry*, 1996; **169** (4): 444–450.

Kemp R, Hayward P and David A. *Compliance Therapy Manual*, London: The Maudsley, 1997.

Kemp R, Hayward P, Grantley A *et al*. Compliance therapy in psychotic patients: Randomised controlled trial. *British Medical Journal*, 1996; 312.

Kemp R, Kirov G, Everitt B *et al*. Randomised controlled trial of compliance therapy. *Br J Psychiatry*, 1998; **172**: 413–419.

Kohn R, Saxena S, Levav I *et al*. The treatment gap in mental health care. *Bull World Health Organisation*, 2004; **82** (11): 858–866.

Kleindienst N and Greil W. Are illness concepts a powerful predictor of adherence to prophylactic treatment in bipolar disorder? *J Clin Psychiatry*, 2004; **65** (7): 966–974.

Kleinman L, Lowin A, Flood E *et al*. Costs of bipolar disorder. *Pharmacoeconomics*, 2003; **21** (9): 601–622.

Knapp M, King D, Punger K *et al*. Non-adherence to antipsychotic medication regimens: Associations with resources use and costs. *Br J Psychiatry*, 2004; **184**: 509–516.

Lacro JP, Dunn LB, Dolder CR *et al*. Prevalence of and risk factors for medication nonadherence in patients with schizophrenia: A comprehensive review of recent literature [cme]. *J Clin Psychiatry*, 2002; **63**: 892–909.

Lam DH. Watkinser, Hayward P *et al*. A randomised controlled study of cognitive therapy for relapse prevention for bipolar affective disorder. *Arch Gen Psychiatry*, 2003; **60**: 145–152.

Lambert M, Conus P, Eide P *et al*. Impact of present and past antipsychotic side effects on attitude toward typical antipsychotic treatment and adherence. *European Psychiatry: The Journal of the Association of European Psychiatrists*, 2004, **19**: (7).

Lecompte D and Pelc I. A cognitive-behavioural program to improve compliance with medication in patients with schizophrenia. *Int J Ment Health*, 1996; **25**: 51–56.

Leff J, Berkowitz R, Shavit N *et al.* A trial of family therapy versus a relatives group for schizophrenia, two year follow-up. *Br J Psychiatry*, 1990; **157**: 571–577.

Leff J, Kuipers L. Berkowitz *et al.* A controlled trial of social interventions in families of schizophrenia patients: Two years follow up. *Br J Psychiatry*, 1985; **146**: 594–600.

Leventhal H, Diefenbach M and Leventhal EA. Illness cognition: Using common sense to understand treatment adherence and affect cognition interactions. *Cognit Ther Res*, 1992; **6**: 143–163.

Ley P. Satisfaction, compliance and communication. *Br J Clin Psychol*, 1982; **21**: 241–254.

Lin EHB, Von Korff M, Katon W *et al.* The role of the primary care physician in patients' adherence to antidepressant therapy. *Med Care*, 1995; **33** (1): 67–74.

Linden M, Godemann F, Gaebel W *et al.* A prospective study of factors influencing adherence to a continuous neuroleptic treatment program in schizophrenia patients during 2 years. *Schizophrenia Bull*, 2001; **27** (4): 585–596.

Lingam R and Scott J. Treatment non-adherence in affective disorders. *Acta Psychiatr Scand*, 2002; **105**: 164–172.

Linszen D, Dingemans P, Van Der Does. *et al.* Treatment, expressed emotion, and relapse in recent onset schizophrenic disorders. *Psychol Med*, 1996; **26**: 333–342.

Liraud F and Verdoux H. Association between temperamental characteristics and medication adherence in subjects presenting with psychotic or mood disorders. *Psychiatry Res*, 2001; **102** (1): 91–95.

Loffler W, Killan R, Toumi M *et al.* Schizophrenic Patients' Subjective – *Pharmacopsychiatry*, 2003; **36** (3): 105–112.

Lowery BJ and DuCette JP. Disease-related learning and disease control in diabetics as a function of locus of control. *Nurs Res*, 1976; **25**: 358–362.

MacPherson R, Jerrom B and Hughes A. A controlled study of education about drug treatment in schizophrenia. *Br J Psychiatry*, 1996; **168**: 709–717.

Mahmoud RA, *et al.* Risperidone versus conventional antipsychotics for schizophrenia and schio affective disorder. *Clinical Drug Investigations*, 2004; **24** (5).

Mander AJ. Is there a lithium withdrawal syndrome? *Br J Psychiatry*, 1986; **149**: 498–501.

Marshall M and Lockwood A. Assertive community treatment for people with severe mental disorders (Cochrane review). *Cohchrane Library*, 2002; **2**.

Mazzuca SA. Does patient education in chronic disease have therapeutic value? *J Chronic Dis*, 1982; **35**: 521–529.

McCabe R and Priebe S. Explanatory models of illness in schizophrenia: Comparison of four ethnic groups. *Br J Psychiatry*, 2004; **185**: 25–30.

McFarlane WR, Lukens E, Link B *et al.* Multiple-family groups and psychoeducation in the treatment of schizophrenia. *Arch Gen Psychiatry*, 1995; **52**: 679–687.

McGavock HA. Review of the literature on drug adherence. *The royal pharmaceutical society of great Britain*, 1996.

Menzin J, Boulanger L, Friedman M *et al.* Treatment adherence associated with conventional and atypical antipsychotics in a large state Medicaid program. *Psychiatr Serv*, 2003; **54** (5): 719–723.

Merinder LB. Patient education in schizophrenia: A review. *Acta Psychiatr Scand*, 2000; **102** (2): 98–106.

Merinder LB, Viuff AG, Laugesen H *et al.* Patient and relative education in community psychiatry; a randomised controlled trial regarding its effectiveness. *Soc Psychiatry Psychiatr Epidemiol*, 1999; **34**: 287–294.

Miklowitz DJ, Goldstein MJ, Nuechterlein KH *et al.* Expresed emotion, affective style, lithium compliance, and relapse in recent onset mania. *Psychopharmacol Bull*, 1986; **22** (3): 628–632.

Miklowitz D, Simoneau T, George E *et al.* Family-focused treatment of bipolar disorder: 1 year effects of a psychoeducational program in condunction with pharmacotherapy. *Biol Psychiatry*, 2000; **48**: 582–592.

Miklowitz DJ, George EL, Richards JA *et al.* A randomised study of family-focused psychoeducation and pharmacotherapy in the outpatient management of bipolar disorder. *Arch Gen Psychiatry*, 2003; **60**: 904–912.

Miller WR and Rollinic S. Motivational interviewing: Preparing people to change addictive behaviour. *Gilford Press*, 1991.

Modrcin M, Rapp CA and Poertner J. The evaluation of case management services with the chronically mentally ill. *Eval Program Plann*, 1988; **11**: 307–314.

Moore A, Sellwood W and Stirling J. Compliance and psychological reactance in schizophrenia. *Br J Clin Psychol*, September 2000; **39** (Pt3): 287–295.

Morselli PL and Elgie R. GAMIAN-Europe*/BEAM survey I. *Bipolar Disord*, 2003; **5**: 265–278.

Mullen PD, Green LW and Persinger GS. Clinical trials of patient education for chronic conditions: A comparative meta-analysis of intervention types. *Prev Med*, November 1985; **14** (6): 753–781.

Mullen PD, Hersey JC and Iverson DC. Health behaviour models compared. *Soc Sci Med*, 1987; **24**: 973–983.

Muller-Oerlinghausen B. Arguments for the specifity of the antisuicidal effect of lithium. *Eur Arch Psychiatry Clin Neurosci*, 2001; **251** (2): II72–1175.

Muller-Oerlinghausen B, Wolf T, Ahrens B *et al.* Mortality of patients who dropped out from regular lithium prophylaxis: A collaborative study by the International Group for the Study of Lithium treated patients (IGSLI). *Acta Psychiatr Scand*, November, 1996; **94** (5): 344–347.

Murray C and Lopez A. The global burden of disease: A comprehensive assessment of mortality and disability from diseases, injuries and risk factors in 1990. Cambridge. MA. Harvard University Press, 1996.

Mutsatsa SH, Joyce EM, Hutton SB *et al.* Clinical correlates of early medication adherence: West London first episode schizophrenia study. *Acta Psychiatr Scand*, December, 2003; **108** (6): 439–446.

Myers L and Midence K. Methodological and conceptual issues in adherence. In: *Adherence to Treatment in Medical Conditions*, 1998:1–24, London: Wiley.

Nelson JC, Schottenfeld RS and Conrad CD. Hypomania after desipramine withdrawal. *Am J Psychiatry*, 1983; **140**: 624–625.

Noble L. Doctor-patient communication and adherence to treatment. In: *Adherence to Treatment in Medical Conditions*, 1998:51–82, London: Wiley.

Nose M, Barbui C and Tansella M. How often do patients with psychosis fail to adhere to treatment programmes? A systematic review. *Psychol Med*, 2003; **33**: 1149–1160.

O'Donnell C, Donohoe G, Sharkey L *et al.* Compliance therapy: A randomised controlled trial in schizophrenia. *British Medical Journal*, 2003: 327.

Olfson M, Mechanic D, Hansell S *et al.* Predicting medication non-compliance after hospital discharge among patients with schizophrenia. *Psychiat Serv*, February 2000; **51** (2): 216–222.

Palmer A and Scott J. Self-management and the expert patient. *Mood Disorders; a Handbook of Science and Practice* (eds) *M. Power*, 2004, John Wiley & Sons, Ltd.

Parson T. *The Social System*, Glencoe: The Free Press.

Patel MX, Young C, Samele C *et al.* Prognostic indicators for early discontinuation of Risperidone long-acting injection. *Int Clin Psychopharmacol*, 2004; **19** (4): 233–239.

Pekkala E and Merinder L. Psychoeducation for schizophrenia. *Cochrane Library of Systematic Reviews*, 2002.

Perlick DA, Rosenheck RA, Kaczynski R *et al.* Medication non-adherence in bipolar disorder: A patient-centered review of research findings. *Clin Approaches Bipolar Disorders*, 2004; **3**: 56–64.

Perry A, Tarrier N, Morris R *et al.* Randomised controlled trial of efficacy of teaching patients with bipolar disorder to identify early symptoms of relapse and obtain treatment. *Br Med J*, 1999; **318**: 149–153.

Peveler R, George C, Kinmouth A *et al.* Effect of antidepressant drug counselling and information leaflets on adherence to drug treatment in primary care: Randomized controlled trial. *Br Med J*, 2000; **319**: 612–615.

Pope M and Scott J. Do clinicians understand why individuals stop taking lithium? *J Affect Disord*, May 2003; **74** (3): 287–291.

Prochaska JO and DiClemente CC. Stages and processes of self-change of smoking: Toward integrative model of change. *J Consult Clin Psychol*, 1983; **51**: 390–395.

Rankin SH and Stallings KD. *Patient education: Issues, principles, practices*, Philadelphia: lippincott-Raven. 1996.

Razali MS and Yahua H. Compliance with treatment in schizophrenia: A drug intervention program in a developing country. *Acta Psychiatr Scand*, 1995; **91**: 331–335.

Razali SM, Hasanah CL, Khan A *et al.* Psychosocial interventions for schizophrenia. *J Ment Health*, 2000; **9**: 283–289.

Rettenbacher MA, Burns T, Kemmler G *et al.* Schizophrenia: Attitudes of patients and professional carers towards the illness and antipsychotic medication. *Pharmacopsychiatry*, 2004b; **37** (3): 103–109.

Rettenbacher MA, Hofer A, Eder U *et al.* Compliance in schizophrenia: Psychopathology, side effects, and patients' attitudes toward the illness and mediation. *J Clin Psychiatry*, 2004a; **65** (9): 1211–1218.

Rice DP. The economic impact of schizophrenia. *J Clin Psychiatry*, 1999; **60**: 4–6.

Rittmannsberger H, Pachinger T. Keppelmuller *et al.* Medication adherence among psychotic patients before admission to inpatient treatment. *Psychiatr Serv*, February 2004; **55** (2): 174–179.

Robinson DG, Woerner MG, Alvir JM *et al.* Predictors of medication discontinuation by patients with first-episode schizophrenia and schizoaffective disorder. *Schizophrenia Res*, October, 2002; **57** (2–3): 209–219.

Robinson P, Bush T, Von Korff M *et al.* Primary care physician use of cognitive behavioural techniques with depressed patients. *J Family Prac*, 1995; **40**: 352–357.

Rollnick S and Miller WR. What is motivational interviewing? Behavioural & cognitive pychotheapy. *Cognit Psychother*, 1995; **23**: 325–334.

Rost K. The influence of patient participation on satisfaction and compliance. *Diabetes Educ*, 1989; **15**: 139–143.

Roter DL, Hall JA, Merisca R *et al.* Effectiveness of interventions to improve patient compliance: A meta-analysis. *Med Care*, 2000; **36**: 1138–1161.

Rotter JB. Generalised expectancies for internal vs. external control of reinforcement. *Psychol Monogr*, 1966; **80**: 1–28.

Rusch N and Corrigan PW. Motivational interviewing to improve insight and treatment adherence in schizophrenia. *Psychiatr Rehabil J*, 2002; **26** (1): 23–32.

Sajatovic M, Davies M, Hrounda D. *et al.* Psychosocial intervention to promote treatment adherence among individuals with bipolar disorder treated in a community setting, 2003.

Sajatovic M, Rosch DS, Sivec HJ *et al.* Insight into illness and attitudes toward medications among inpatients with schizophrenia. *Psychiatr Serv*, October 2002; **53** (10): 1319–1324.

Schooler NR, Keith SJ, Stevere JB *et al.* Relapse and rehospitalisation during maintenance treatment of schizophrenia: The effects of dose reduction and family treatment. *Arch Gen Psychiatry*, 1997; **54**: 453–463.

Schou M. The combat of non-compliance during prophylactic lithium treatment. *Acta Psychiatr Scand*, 1997; **95**: 361–363.

Schumann C, Lenz G, Berghofer A *et al.* Non-adherence with long-term prophylaxis: A 6-year naturalistic follow-up study of affectively ill patients. *Psychiatry Res*, 1999; **89**: 247–257.

Scott J. Psychotherapy for bipolar disorder. *Br J Psychiatry*, 1995; **167**: 581–588.

Scott J. Cognitive and behavioural approaches to medication adherence. *Adv Psychiatric Treatment*, 1999; **5**: 338–347.

Scott J. Predicting medication non-adherence in severe affective disorders. *Acta Neurolopsychiatrica*, 2000; **12**: 128–130.

Scott J and Colom F. Psychological treatments for bipolar disorders. *Psychiatr Clin North Am*, 2005; **28**: 371–384.

Scott J and Pope M. Self-reported adherence to treatment with mood stabilizers, plasma levels, and psychiatric hospitalization. *Am J Psychiatry*, November, 2002a; **159** (11): 1927–1929.

Scott J and Pope M. Non-adherence with mood stabilisers: Prevalence and predictors. *J Clin Psychol*, 2002b; **63**: 384–390.

Scott J and Tacchi MJ. A pilot study of concordance therapy for individuals with bipolar disorder who are non-adherent with lithium prophylaxis. *Bipolar Disord*, 2002; **4**: 286–293.

Scott J and Wright J. Cognitive therapy for severe mental disorders. In: *Review of Psychiatry*, 1997; **16**: 135–170. Washington DC: Apa Press.

Sellwood W, Tarrier N, Quinn J. *et al*. The family and compliance in schizophrenia: The influence of clinical variables, relatives' knowledge and expressed emotion. *Psychol Med*, January; **2003** (1): 91–96.

Seltzer A, Roncar I and Garfinkel P. Effect of patient education on medication compliance. *Can J Psychiatry*, 1980; **25**: 638–645.

Shakir AS, Fred R, Volkmar MD *et al*. Group psychotherapy as an adjunct to lithium maintenance. *Am J Psychiatry*, 1979; **136**: 455–456.

Smith DL. Compliance packaging: A patient education tool. *Am Pharm*, 1989; Ns29 (2): 42–45, 49–53.

Smith J, Birchwood M and Haddrell A. Informing people with schizophrenia about their illness: The effect of residual symptoms. *J Ment Health*, 1992; (1) 61–70.

Smith TE, Hull JW, Goodman M *et al*. The relative influences of symptoms, insight, and neurocognition on social adjustment in schizophrenia and schizoaffective disorder. *J Nerv Ment Dis*, 1999; **187**: 102–108.

Solomon P and Draine J. The efficacy of a consumer case management team: 2-year outcomes of a randomised trial. *J Ment Health Adm*, 1995; **22**: 135–146.

Stein LI and Test MA. Alternative to mental hospital treatment, I: Conceptual model, treatment program, and clinical evaluation. *Arch Gen Psychiatry*, 1980; **37**: 392–397.

Stephenson BJ, Rowe BH, Haynes RB *et al*. Is this patient taking the treatment as prescribed? *J Am Med Assoc*, 1993; **269**: 2779–2781.

Streicker SK, Amdur M and Dincin J. Educating patients about psychiatric medications: Failure to enhance compliance. *Psychosoc Rehabil J*, 1986; **4**: 15–28.

Svarstad B. The patient-physician encounter: An observational study of communication and outcome. 1974.

Svarstad BL, Shireman TI and Sweeney JK. Using drug claims data to assess the relationship of medication adherence with hospitalisation and costs. *Psychiatr Serv*, 2001; **52**: 805–811.

Swartz M, Swanson J, Hiday V *et al*. Violence and severe mental illness: The effects of substance misuse and non-adherence to medication. *Am J Psychiatry*, 1998; **155**: 226–231.

Tarrier N and Barrowclough C. Professional attitudes to psychiatric patients: A time for change and an end to medication parenalism. *Epidemiol Psichiatr Soc*, 2003; **12** (4): 238–241.

Tarrier N, Barrowclough C, Vaughan C *et al*. The community management of schizophrenia. A controlled trial of a behavioural intervention with families to reduce relapse. *Br J Psychiatry*, 1988; **153**: 532–542.

Tattan TM and Creed FH. Negative symptoms of schizophrenia and compliance with medication. *Schizophrenia BullI*, 2001; **27** (1): 149–155.

Telles C, Karno M, Mintz J *et al*. Immigrant families coping with schizophrenia. *Br J Psychiatry*, 1995; **167**: 473–479.

Thieda P, Beard S, Richer A *et al*. An economic review of compliance with medication therapy in the treatment of schizophrenia. *Psychiatr Serv*, 2003; **54** (4): 508–516.

Tohen M, Greil W, Calabrese JR *et al*. Olanzapine versus lithium in the maintenance treatment of bipolar disorder: American Journal of Psychiatry, 2005; **162** (7): 1281–1290.

Tohen M, Griel W, Calabrese JR *et al*. Olanzapine versus lithium in the maintenance treatment of bipolar disorder: A 12-month, randomised, double-blind, controlled clinical trial. *Am J Psychiatry* 2005; **162**: 1281–1290.

Traver T and Sacks T. The relationship between insight and medication adherence in severely mentally ill clients treated in the community. *Acta Psychiatr Scand*, 2000; **102**: 211–216.

Valenstein M, Copeland LA, Owen R *et al*. Adherence assessments and the use of depot antipsychotics in patients with schizophrenia. *J Clin Psychiatry* July 2001; **62** (7): 545–551.

Van Gent C and Zwart F. Psycho-education of partners of bipolar-manic patients. *J Affect Disord*, 1991; **21**: 15–18.

Van Putten T, Crumpton E and Yale C. Drug refusal in schizophrenia and the wish to be crazy. *Arch Gen Psychiatry*, 1976; **33**: 1433–1446.

Vauth R, Loschmann C, Rusch N *et al*. Understanding adherence to neuroleptic treatment in schizophrenia. *Psychiatry Res*, April 2004; **126** (1): 43–49.

Velligan DI, Bow-Thomas CC, Huntzinger CD *et al*. A randomised controlled trial of the use of compensatory strategies in schizophrenic outpatients. *Am J Psychiatry*, 2000; **157**: 1317–1323.

Velligan DI, Lam F, Ereshefsky L *et al*. Psychopharmacology: Perspectives on medication adherence and atypical antipsychotic medications. *Psychiatr Serv*, May 2003; **54** (5): 665–667.

Weiden P and Havens L. Psychotherapeutic management techniques in the treatment of outpatients with schizophrenia. *Hosp Community Psychiatry*, 1994; **45** (6): 549–555.

Weiden PJ and Olfson M. Cost of relapse in schizophrenia. *Schizophrenia Bull*, 1995; **21**(3): 419–429.

Weiden P, Aquila R and Standard J. Atypical antipsychotic drugs and long-term outcome in schizophrenia. *J Clin Psychiatry*, 1996; **11**: 53–60.

Weiden PJ, Kozma C, Grogg A *et al*. Partial compliance and risk of rehospitalisation among California Medicaid patients with schizophrenia. *Psychiatr Serv*, August, 2004; **55** (8): 886–891.

Weiden P, Rapkin B, Zygmunt A *et al*. Post discharge medication compliance of inpatients converted from an oral to a depot neuroleptic regimen. *Psychiatr Serv*, 1995; **46**: 1049–1054.

Weinstein ND. The precaution adoption process. *Health Psychol*, 1988; **7**: 355–386.

Weiss KA, Smith TE, Hull JW *et al*. Predictors of risk of nonadherence in outpatients with schizophrenia and other psychotic disorders. *Schizophrenia Bull*, 2002; **28** (2): 341–349.

World Health Organization. *Adherence to Long-Term Therapies: Evidence for Action* World Health Organization. 2003.

Wright E. Non-compliance – or how many aunts has Matilda? *Lancet*, 1993; **342**: 909–913.

Wyatt RJ and Henter I. The economic evaluation of manic-depressive illness 1991. *Social psychiatry and psychiatric epidemiology*, 1995; **30**: 213–219.

Wyatt RJ, Henter ID and Jamison JC. Lithium revisited: Savings brought about by the use of lithium, 1970–1991. *Psychiatr Q*, 2001; **72** (2): 149–166.

Xiang M and Ran M. A controlled evaluation of psychoeducational family intervention in a rural Chinese community. *Br J Psychiatry* 1994; **165**: 544–548.

Xiang W, Phillips MR, Xiong H *et al*. A family-based intervention for schizophrenic patients in China: A randomised controlled trial. *Br J Psychiatry*, 1994; **165**: 239–247.

Zhang M, Wang M, Li J *et al*. Randomised-control trial of family intervention for 78 first episode male schizophrenic patients; an 18-month study in Suzhou, Jiangsu. *Br J Psychiatry Suppl*, 1994; **24**: 96–102.

Zygmunt A, Olfson M, Boyer CA *et al*. Interventions to improve medication adherence in schizophrenia. *Am J Psychiatry*, October 2002; **159** (10): 1653–1664.

Index